DAVID LOWE CHICAGO INTERIORS

DAVID LOWE CHICAGO INTERIORS

VIEWS OF A SPLENDID WORLD

CONTEMPORARY BOOKS, INC.   CHICAGO 1979

Endpapers: View of Chicago as seen from Lake Michigan in 1928. Drawing by H. M. Pettit.

Title Page: An unfailing way to create a sense of splendor in an interior is by arranging a series of rooms enfilade. David Adler did just that in the house he designed on Astor Street in 1921 for Joseph T. Ryerson. This photograph was taken from the drawing room looking towards the dining room.

Library of Congress Cataloging in Publication Data

Lowe, David
   Chicago interiors.

   Includes index.
   1. Architecture—Illinois—Chicago.   2. Chicago—
Buildings.   3. Interior decoration—Illinois—Chicago.
I. Title.
NA735.C4L67   1979   720'.9773'11   78-57442
ISBN 0-8092-5992-3

Published by Contemporary Books, Inc.
180 North Michigan Avenue, Chicago, Illinois 60601
Manufactured in the United States of America
Library of Congress Catalog Card Number: 78-57442
International Standard Book Number: 0-8092-5992-3

Published simultaneously in Canada by
Beaverbooks
953 Dillingham Road
Pickering, Ontario L1W 1Z7
Canada

For my mother, Grace Dexter Garrard,
who loved shopping on State Street,
watching the races at Washington Park,
and dancing at the Edgewater Beach Hotel

This elegant fleur-de-lis *was one of the patterns specified by
Louis Sullivan for the mosaic floor of the Auditorium Hotel lobby
of 1889.*

There seems to me no observable tendencies
in the American mind to a form of national
character which will be content with one
type of architecture

JOHN WELLBORN ROOT, 1887

*A fireplace showing an unmistakable Moorish influence was
designed by John Wellborn Root in 1885 for the Edward E. Ayer
house, Two East Banks Street.*

CONTENTS

PREFACE

One summer afternoon when I was ten or eleven years of age, I wandered with a cousin among the Oxfordian spires of the University of Chicago. By chance, or rather by good luck, I stepped inside the university's Rockefeller Memorial Chapel. The vastness of that Gothic Mammoth Cave stunned me. "There is so much more inside than out," I said. I know those were my words, for my cousin, who was older and therefore supposedly wiser, repeated them with appropriate laughter for years afterwards. But there *was* more inside. The exterior, as anyone who has seen it knows, of Bertram Goodhue's Protestant cathedral bulks large indeed, but it is as nothing when compared to that long nave, those high vaults, that richness of tall stained glass, that sense, above all, of voluminous space enclosed. Coming upon Chartres across the flat plain of the Ile de France is a rare and moving experience, but to fully understand the potency of the Virgin's shrine, one must enter its portals.

After I had written *Lost Chicago,* I often wondered what the interiors of certain structures in that book looked like. What, for instance, had been the appearance of the council chamber in James J. Egan's grandiose post-fire City Hall, and what was the form of the bar in that nineteenth-century lair of La Salle Street traders, the Grand Pacific Hotel? Two buildings in particular intrigued me: the Palmer House of 1873 and the Central Music Hall of 1879. I had read the raptures of visitors concerning the hotel's restaurant—not to be confused with its grand dining room—but other than a mediocre print, I had discovered no visual record of it. As for the Central Music Hall, the question of the design of that auditorium, which had first brought together Dankmar Adler and Louis Sullivan, haunted me.

The temptation to compile a volume on Chicago interiors was thus very strong, but my experience in picture archives made me realize how difficult it is to find good interior views. The Central Music Hall, for example, appears in dozens of 1880s and 1890s panoramas of State Street, but photographers in those decades did not casually step inside buildings and snap their shutters. In the first place, there was always the problem of proper lighting; in the second, if a photographer did snap an interior it was most likely to photograph a speaker or a ceremony. That was usually not the type of photograph I wanted.

Yet, as it often does, temptation won out. The work was, if I may say so, arduous but the rewards were sometimes astonishing. The descendants of the families who had built some of Chicago's great houses came forward with albums showing the rooms as they had looked the day the occupants moved in. In the depths of the picture collection of the Library of Congress in Washington, I found the ornate council chamber of James J. Egan's City Hall; in the basement files of the Burnham Library of the Art Institute, I had my first blissful glimpse of Adler and Sullivan's Central Music Hall. But it was in London that the proverbial lightning struck.

One day in a shop that dealt in old photographs, I was browsing through a bin of stereopticon slides marked "The States" when my eye fell on one that recalled a print I had seen. I picked it up and there inscribed on the back was "Restaurant of the Palmer House hotel, Chicago." In that moment I knew how Howard Carter had felt that day in 1922 when he discovered Tutankhamen's tomb. Looking at that marbled, mirrored magnificence, I wondered what English visitor had carried it home across the Atlantic to be preserved through the sorting out that follows death, and through the Blitz, to be once more resurrected in its home city.

My search, as it slowly bore fruit, was a revelation in still another way. Along with my doubts concerning the availability of good photographs, I had feared that those I did find might prove to have too little variety to add up to an interesting book. This fear, fortunately, turned out to be totally unfounded. Writing in the *Inland Architect and News Record* of March 1887, the architect John Wellborn Root predicted:

> The tremendous and rapidly acquired wealth, not only of individuals but of the nation as a whole, coupled as it is by no national indifference to display, and by no national parsimony, will inevitably lead to the erection of buildings, both of private, commercial, and public character, whose splendor will be phenomenal in the history of the world.

Nowhere, I discovered, was there less parsimony, nowhere less indifference to display than in Chicago, and nowhere was the splendor more incandescent. Looking at the photographs of the interiors of the Potter Palmer castle I was struck anew by the sheer bravado of the city. Perhaps Anne O'Hare McCormick summed it up best in a brilliant piece she wrote for the *New York Times* contrasting the 1932 Republican and Democratic conventions, both of which were held in the Windy City that year: "Chicago," Miss McCormick said, "is the ideal location for dancing on top of a volcano. Eruptive and exciting, a city of superlatives, it exaggerates all the splendor and squalor of America." Potter and Bertha Honoré Palmer certainly went in for the splendor. The size of their entrance hall, the Rothschildian display of their dining table, the carefully premeditated glitter of their drawing room was matched in no more than a dozen houses in America. And then, to still any derisive laughter before it began, there was the picture gallery, filled with those breathtaking Monets and Degas and Renoirs like so many words adding up to the statement: "Don't say we didn't know what we were doing."

As this book grew so did my respect for those Chicago architects whose work I already knew quite well: Louis Sullivan, William Boyington, Frank Lloyd Wright, George W. Maher, Howard Van Doren Shaw, and John Wellborn Root. But I also gained new respect for architects whose work I had known less well: Benjamin Marshall, creator of the exotic Edgewater Beach Hotel; Alfred S. Alschuler, who raided Byzantium for his Temple Isaiah; and Solon S. Beman, building in his train shed of Grand Central Station a wonderful stable for iron horses. Then—and this was especially rewarding—there were new names: August Fiedler, the man behind the Gemutlichkeit of Henrici's restaurant; and Charles H. Prindiville whose St. Jerome's Church is a Renaissance-style glory. What a cloud of witnesses to good building Chicago has had!

Enhancing the work of the architects, giving color to their walls, texture to their ceilings, furnishings for their rooms, there were, I discovered, a small army of painters, designers, and decorators. It is now impossible for me to look at the Auditorium without thinking of the muralist Louis J. Millet who worked so closely with Sullivan there. To step inside Ralph Adams Cram's Fourth Presbyterian Church is to be reminded of the endearing artist, Frederic C. Bartlett, whose handiwork that richly polychromed ceiling is. The old Art Deco Tavern Club will always call to mind Johns Hopkins of the decorating department of Holabird and Root, while the elegant Fortnightly belongs to that subtle decorator, Mrs. John Alden Carpenter, and the bright memory of the dismantled Pump Room will be Samuel Marx's most enduring monument.

In the course of my research all of these people became astonishingly alive to me. When that noble organization, The Cliff Dwellers, produced a picture of Louis Sullivan sitting in one of their rooms, I felt that I could easily strike up a conversation with the master. When I saw a photograph of the Adam-inspired dining room of the Pearson Hotel I knew why it was more truly ritzy than the Ritz which had succeeded to its place, for its architect, Robert De Golyer, had been the spirit behind the charms of that demolished North Michigan Avenue delight, the Italian Court.

There was, I became increasingly aware as I read more and more about Chicago, an abiding fascination with its physical presence, its sticks and stones, its bricks and mortar on the part of its poets and novelists. Time and again, like a living character, it enters their work. No doubt this is because so many of them came from those little one-horse Midwestern towns that have so profoundly shaped the character of America's heartland. The magnitude of Chicago, for them, was something new, something slightly startling, something that forever lodged in their imaginations. This was true for Theodore Dreiser from Warsaw, Indiana; for Sherwood Anderson from Clyde, Ohio; for Edgar Lee Masters from Lewistown, Illinois; for Carl Sandburg from Galesburg, Illinois; for Willa Cather from Red Cloud, Nebraska. Whenever possible I brought in the words of the Chicago writers. For me they made certain scenes reverberate.

When I began this project I had no intention of writing another "lost" book. But, alas, few things are more fragile than interiors. Buildings might remain, but in a strange reversal of the habit of the serpent, they shed not their skins but their innards. So while many of the structures whose rooms are shown here have vanished entirely—the Pearson Hotel, the Franklin MacVeagh house, the Great Northern Theatre—others, such as the public rooms of the still-standing Congress Hotel, have been lost to a misdirected enthusiasm for "modernization." Thankfully, others survive intact or almost intact: the Rockefeller Chapel, The Cliff Dwellers Club, and The Chicago Public Library. My criterion for a room or a structure's inclusion in this book was not that it was lost or not lost, but that it was in some way, to my eyes, beautiful.

The mention of the word "beautiful" forces me to come to its defense, for the question will undoubtedly be raised as to why I did not include the ugly side of Chicago in this book, why not the tenements with the mansions, why not the slaughterhouses with the Stockyards Inn? My answer is simple: that was not the task I set for myself. In a curious, almost masochistic turn of mind, Americans too often seem to be ashamed of their country's triumphs. This book celebrates the triumph of a city, the triumph of splendor. It celebrates a city that had public delights of the caliber of the Tivoli Theatre, and private ones of the subtlety of the Edward Ayer house; a city that had temples of commerce of the grandeur of the Continental Illinois Bank, and temples of worship of the perfection of Frank Lloyd Wright's Unity. This book unashamedly measures the civilization of Chicago by the heights it reached.

In that sometimes exasperating but always interesting collection of essays, *Kindergarten Chats,* Louis Sullivan proved that the genius who could so deftly draw a design could just as easily pen a poem. One of his poems begins:

Here lies a valley in the heart of summer!
Kine in shadows,
Crops in dazzling light.
Dreamy and still this air;
All songsters hushed . . .

Here is Chicago in summer; here is Chicago in dazzling light. The songsters who created these rooms are hushed, but ah, what a song they sang.

DAVID LOWE

Louis Sullivan, in his most inventive vein, is revealed in this cast-iron medallion from an elevator grill on the main floor of Carson, Pirie, Scott, and Company. The Art Nouveau piece, fabricated by Winslow Brothers of Chicago, dates from 1903 or 1904.

Frank Lloyd Wright's drawing of the bookshop he completed for Francis Browne in 1908 on the seventh floor of the Fine Arts Building shows why Margaret Anderson, who worked there, called it "the most beautiful bookshop in the world." Anderson, who was to become famous as the founder of The Little Review, described the shop in detail in her memoir My Thirty Years' War: "The walls were rough cement, sand color; the bookshelves, shoulder high, were in the form of stalls, each containing a long reading table and easy chairs." The delightful shop, where, in the palmy days of Chicago's literary renaissance just before World War I, afternoon tea was likely to attract Sherwood Anderson, Floyd Dell, Maxwell Bodenheim, and Edgar Lee Masters, has been dismantled.

ACKNOWLEDGMENTS

Any list of acknowledgments of those who helped with this book must begin with the name of Carl D. Brandt of Brandt and Brandt who was always there when an encouraging word was needed.

I would like to thank next in order Annette Fern and Marion Knoblauch-Franc, whose help with the research for this project was never less than magnificent.

In the gathering of the illustrations for this book I was constantly touched and amazed by the kindness and helpfulness of almost all of those connected with the archives in which I worked. Let me first cite the Burnham Library of Architecture of the Art Institute of Chicago and its librarian, Daphne C. Roloff, and her assistants, Deborah Ezzio and Cecilia Chin. I would also like to thank the library's architectural archivist, John Zukowsky. The staff of the Prints and Photographs Division of the Library of Congress in Washington gave willingly of their time and knowledge, particularly Jerry Kearns, head of the reference section, and C. Ford Peatross, curator of the architectural collections. The New York Historical Society proved enthusiastic concerning this project on a sister city, and the Print Room there was a rich source of material. Let me thank Mary Black of that institution. The Picture Collection of the New York Public Library was another source of unexpected treasures; its staff was never less than gracious. Finally, any book on Chicago must make a bow in the direction of the Chicago Historical Society. Julia Westerberg of the Society's Graphics Department once more showed herself both wise and caring.

I am under a particular obligation to two men who possess a rare awareness of all the subtleties of the photograph. Harold Allen, a photographer who has had a long love affair with Chicago, is the eye and hand behind some of the finest illustrations in this volume. Jack O. Hedrich, head of Hedrich-Blessing, opened his firm's files to me, and is thus responsible for many of the high-quality photographs of the 1920s, '30s, '40s, and '50s found on these pages. Let me also thank Gary M. Knaus of that firm. Along with these two men I would like to mention a kindred spirit, Robert Jackson, president of Culver Pictures of New York, who made available to me the resources of that treasure-trove of images on paper.

A special group who provided rare and wonderful things because of their special connections with Chicago deserve a deep bow indeed. Let me name Sir Harold Acton, Rhea Adler, Edward Morris Bakwin, Ruth Morris Bakwin, Muriel Morris Buttinger, Charles Dishman, Bertrand and Nancy Goldberg, Marjorie Goodman Graff, John A. Holabird, Jr., James Fulton Hoge, Jr., Byron C. Karzas, and Lila Hotz Tyng.

I wish also to thank those Chicago firms and institutions that so graciously opened their files to me: the *Chicago Daily News,* the *Chicago Tribune,* The Cliff Dwellers, the Commission on Chicago Historical and Architectural Landmarks, Grace Protestant Episcopal Church, Henrici's, Marshall Field and Company, the Medinah Temple, the Palmer House, C. D. Peacock Jewelers, the Scottish Rite Cathedral, the Standard Club, and the Washington Park Jockey Club.

I would be more than a little remiss if I did not mention those who, in various but important ways, have encouraged this task: Timothy Field Beard, Richard H. Brown, Esther Bubley, John Cadenhead, Forrest F. Carhart, Jr., Ferdinand W. Coudert, Richard and Moira Du Brul, Paul Gapp, Donald P. Gurney, Sally Forbes, David Hanks, Ruth Page, and William Seale.

Let me thank too Howard Solotroff who was the art director for this book.

The words on these pages owe an enormous debt of gratitude to the Avery Architectural Library at Columbia University and to its director, Adolph Placzek. I would also like to acknowledge my debt to the Joseph Regenstein Library of the University of Chicago. No thanks can begin to repay the help given to me at the New York Public Library by the staffs of the Local History and Genealogy and of the Art rooms. I also wish to express my gratitude to the library for the use of the Frederick Lewis Allen Room. In Chicago, my base of research was the Newberry Library and more than a word of appreciation is due that institution and the librarians of its special collections.

No list of acknowledgments for this book would be complete without "une grande merci" to Charles Durand of Durand Ruel et Cie of Paris, who for two weeks permitted me to peruse that great picture gallery's correspondence and thus to begin to comprehend Chicago's French connection.

—D. L.

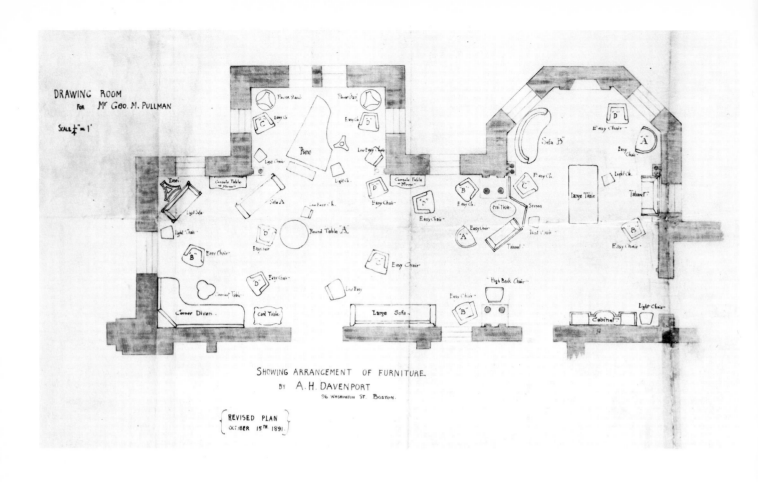

DRAWING ROOM
FOR Mr Geo. M. Pullman

SCALE ¼" = 1'

SHOWING ARRANGEMENT OF FURNITURE.
BY A.H. DAVENPORT
96 WASHINGTON ST. BOSTON.

REVISED PLAN
OCTOBER 15TH 1891.

*This scheme for the placement of the furniture in the drawing
room of George M. Pullman's Prarie Avenue mansion was made
by the Boston decorator A. H. Davenport.*

INTRODUCTION

There is a drawing in the archives of the Chicago Historical Society that reveals as much about the relationship between architecture and decoration in the nineteenth century as would several weighty tomes on the subject. This illuminating document is the revised plan of October 15, 1891 for the placement of the furniture in George M. Pullman's drawing room. The plan was contrived by A. H. Davenport, decorator, of Boston, Massachusetts. There, with unmistakable clarity, if no great artistry, every piece is put in its proper place, or at least in what the decorator thought was its proper place. To guarantee that Mr. Pullman would make no gaffes—heaven forbid!—each item is boldly labeled: "Cloverleaf Table," "Card Table," "Console Table," "Easy Chair A" and "B" and "C" and "D." One is left with the uncomfortable feeling that the furniture might very well have been nailed down.

This is an astonishing document, for George Mortimer Pullman was no ordinary mortal. He had perfected that monument of mobile domesticity, the sleeping car; he had organized America's first modern corporation; he had constructed America's pioneering company town. In 1890, the year before he was so summarily told where to put his easy chairs, the Pullman Palace Car Company, of which he was president, had a total revenue of nearly $9,000,000, employed some 12,000 people, and had carried more than five million passengers in its 2,135 cars. Yet here is George Pullman, so concerned about being correct in the arrangement of his drawing room, that he hires a decorator to sketch, as it were, a map for him.

What makes this document especially revealing is that Mr. Pullman engaged a decorator for the task, not an architect. It was not as though Mr. Pullman did not know an architect. He had had a long and most cordial working relationship with a first-rate one, Solon S. Beman. Beman had not been the architect of George Pullman's brownstone Prairie Avenue chateau when it was built in 1873; that had been the work of John M. Dunphy. But Beman had made some important additions to the mansion; and it was he who designed the splendid Romanesque Pullman Building on Michigan Avenue where George Pullman had his office; and it was Solon Beman who created the town of Pullman just south of Chicago where the marvelous Pullman cars were built. Yet George M. Pullman did not go to Solon S. Beman to have his drawing room refurbished, and that is what it was, a refurbishing, with a good deal of 1890s white and gold splashed over the somber 1870s walnut woodwork which suddenly looked old-fashioned.

George Pullman's desire to be à la page seems to be an inborn trait of Western man. In 1144 when the Abbé Suger completed the rebuilding of the royal burial place of St. Denis on the outskirts of Paris in the new Gothic style, he made all the old Romanesque churches of Europe suddenly appear passé. Bishops and archbishops, mother superiors and abbesses flocked to St. Denis like so many department store buyers at a Dior opening, studied the ribbed vaulting, and then rushed home to have it copied. Perhaps there is no more telling example of this passion to be à la mode than St. Peter's in Rome. When at the beginning of the sixteenth century Pope Julius II decided to demolish the basilica raised by the Emperor Constantine more than 1,000 years earlier, the reason he gave for his destruction of what was undoubtedly the most revered shrine in Christendom was that the walls were unsafe. The real reason though, was that the pope wanted an up-to-date church in the new "High Renaissance" style by the fashionable architect Donato Bramante. St. Denis and St. Peter's reveal, not only man's unquenchable thirst for the novel in architecture and decoration, but also the fact that in both cases—that is, with the anonymous masons who flocked to help the Abbé Suger and with Bramante—the architect and the decorator were one and the same.

This state of affairs remained true until the beginning of the eighteenth century. At that time the growing wealth of Western Europe, the increasing contact with the Orient, and the first faint stirrings of the Industrial Revolution led to a multiplication of the types of furniture and fabrics available. Suddenly the treatment of everything from windows to doors grew ever more complex and rooms were, for the first time, devised for specific uses such as dining. This last development was nothing less than revolutionary.

Therefore it is not surprising that it is in the eighteenth century when we have two men, Robert

Adam and William Kent, whose names begin the history of English decoration. Adam, a Scot who journeyed to Italy and there fell in love with the debris of ancient Rome, returned to Britain to promote neo-classical taste. Among his numerous contributions to decoration was his use of colored drawings to show his clients exactly how the furniture in their rooms should be arranged. If Adam did not invent the idea, he most certainly was the first important architect-decorator to use it consistently. He was, in fact, the progenitor of that artless drawing done for Mr. Pullman. Adam, of course, did not just make the plans for the arrangement of the furniture in rooms, he also designed the furniture and the rooms and the houses that contained them. In some cases, it is only fair to say, he left a few details to his favorite cabinet maker, Thomas Chippendale. But when one visits Kedleston in Derbyshire or Syon House near London one has the sense of "Adam" having been indelibly stamped on everything.

Kent, like Robert Adam, was a complete architect-decorator. Typically, in a great house such as Houghton in Norfolk, his hand and eye created the tables and armchairs, the settees and beds, the pedestals and candelabras, as well as the fabrics which covered the walls. Indeed, so involved did William Kent become with these things, that the term "to decorate" was coined to describe his work. The term was not without a certain pejorative connotation. In a famous remark uttered in 1787, the great Dr. Samuel Johnson, the father of the English dictionary, averred, while speaking of Kent and the architect John James, "James and Kent were mere decorators." Dr. Johnson was not an easy man to please and the blunt lexicographer did not use his new word kindly. Yet to enter a creation by William Kent such as the superb townhouse he designed at 44 Berkeley Square in London is to know that one is in the presence of more than a "mere decorator." The truest equivalent to Adam and Kent in America was Thomas Jefferson, who at Monticello built a house that in every detail bespoke the intentions of its architect.

In the last decade of the eighteenth century, the increase in the multiplicity of styles and types of furniture and fabrics, which had been noted at the beginning of the century, rapidly accelerated. The Industrial Revolution was getting under full steam, bringing with it by the 1820s a cornucopia of mass-produced furniture, materials, and the blissful possibility that every mantle in every home could be garnished with a brass statuette of the Venus de Milo with a clock in her stomach. Great Britain and the United States were about to enter the Victorian era, a period whose interior decoration may be characterized as being one long romance with infinite variety. In the wake of this explosion of decorative possibilities architects lost control over the interiors of the structures they designed.

In England, the first people who may be characterized exclusively as "decorators" were, in fact, upholsterers. They dealt with what was by far the most costly aspect of fitting up a house, and it soon became customary to give the upholsterers full payment for the entire job and allow them in turn to hire the craftsmen needed to carry out the other tasks. In France, as might be expected of the nation that had devised the rigid etiquette of the court of Versailles, the matter was quickly regularized with interior decoration controlled by *marchands merciers,* entrepreneurs who had charge over the *ébénistes* or cabinet makers, the *menuisiers* who made seat furniture, and the *tapissiers* who were responsible for the upholstery.

The new position of the architect caught in this veritable avalanche of gimp and fringe is vividly illustrated by the case of Sir Jeffry Wyatville who, while rebuilding portions of Windsor Castle in the late 1820s, informed his patron, no less a personage than George IV, that others must finish the interiors of the castle since that was not his province. Just how complicated a proposition this had become is revealed in a book published in London in 1840, *The House Decorator and Painter's Guide,* by H. W. and A. Arrowsmith who gloried in the designation of "decorators to Her Majesty." H. W. and A. Arrowsmith show by means of colored illustrations some of the more popular styles of the day for interiors. The list includes: Elizabethan, Greek, Pompeiian, Louis XIV, Louis XV, Francis I, Arabesque, Etruscan, Moorish, and Venetian. No wonder Sir Jeffry begged to be excused from doing up George IV's rooms!

Chicago is a child of the nineteenth century, of the Victorian era, of the Industrial Revolution. In its infancy the smoke of factory chimneys was its blanket, the noonday whistle its lullaby. There is no doubt that, when John Van Osdel built the city's first architect-designed house on Ontario Street for William Butler Ogden in 1836-37, he fully concurred with Sir Jeffry and left the matter of decorating its interiors to others. We know that most of the furnishings in Ogden's house came, as he did, from the east and that its rooms were painted by one of the twenty-or-so specialists in frescoing who had already established himself in the prairie boom town.

Chicago did not have to wait long, though, for some of these painters and glazers to emerge as so-called decorators. In 1840 S. S. Barry and Son was established by Samuel Stedman Barry. The firm flourished, for in the decade after the Great Fire of 1871, S. S. Barry had a grand total of 150 employees. Among the city's most respected early decorators was Thomas Nelson who began working in Chicago in 1853. The commission he received to carry out the painting, glazing, and frescoing of the post-fire County Building was by far the largest such contract up to that time in the city's history.

An almost insurmountable obstacle for those Chicagoans wishing to beautify their homes in the first half of the nineteenth century was the paucity of places to buy furniture or fabrics. Among the prosperous classes this led to frequent excursions to the emporiums of New York and Boston, but this was not always practicable and, besides, one could not make a several-hundred-mile journey every time a bolt of cloth or a roll of wallpaper was needed.

Cloth and wallpaper, it seems, were crucial. Chicago had gained the reputation as being so desperate for these items that it became the dumping ground for any atrocious design that had failed to sell elsewhere. In 1853 this situation was remedied by the founding of Faxon's, eventually located on Wabash Avenue. The firm's advertisements promised: "Art paper hangings in all the latest designs and colorings in fine and medium priced goods," and went on to note that "With a first-class corps of competent workmen, we are prepared to decorate every home in the most appropriate manner and at the lowest prices." In its early years the store's motto "The One and Only Faxon" was felt by most Chicagoans not to be an exaggeration.

The city's growing population and its increasing prosperity soon attracted more and more establishments which catered to those desiring a John Henry Belter rococo revival sofa or a Cornelius gaselier. The 1868 *Guide to the City of Chicago* is a revealing index of this proliferation. Steurer and Robinson at 190 Lake Street, for instance, offered fashionable parlor suites in a choice of rosewood, black walnut, or mahogany, as well as "library things." Field, Leiter, and Company, also on Lake Street, was stocked with "paper, upholstery, and oil cloth" and was particularly proud of its Aubusson-inspired Brussels and Wilton pile carpets. As an indication of just how far matters had progressed, Johnson and Cobb at 152 Lake Street limited themselves to specializing in slip covers.

The pre-fire houses decorated by S. S. Barry, Thomas Nelson, and others were, on the whole, surprisingly unpretentious in their furnishings. When looking at old photographs of these dwellings, such as the one Leander McCormick, brother of the great Cyrus, built on Rush Street in 1863, one senses a certain frugality. To be sure they are comfortable and the best parlor inevitably boasts a carved white marble fireplace, topped by a gilded mirror, and its floor is covered by a profusely flowered carpet, but there is a sense here that possessions are still considered precious, as though the owners of the houses remembered back to the days before the Industrial Revolution made possible Grecian sideboards, Gothic bookcases, and gold-colored French chairs in almost infinite number. These spare rooms seem from a time earlier than the 1860s, they seem to belong to the 1820s. Perhaps it was just that Chicago's new rich did not yet fully realize just how rich they were.

The atmosphere of these somewhat Spartan houses is wonderfully evoked in Janet Ayer Fairbank's 1925 novel *The Smiths:*

> After supper they sat, as usual, in the tiny front parlor, where a glass lamp stood on the exact center of the marble topped table. . . . A black walnut sofa was placed in the exact center of the side wall. . . . The two armchairs which went with it were drawn to the table and the lamp. Between the windows a "what-not" stood, on which were set out the family ornaments.

A far more sumptuous world was about to be born.

One of the first mentions in print in Chicago of decorators actually at work appeared in the *Chicago Tribune* on October 8, 1871 in a description of the new Crosby's Opera House on Washington Street. "The decorators and upholsterers," the newspaper reported, "are still busy putting the finishing touches on the Opera House." They might have saved their effort, for the Great Fire would put the finishing touches on Crosby's the very next day.

The Chicago which re-emerged after that holocaust had none of the reticence of the pre-fire city. New decorative styles bloomed like unexpected desert flowers after a downpour. Among the most popular were "Italian Renaissance" and "advanced or modern Gothic." Alfred T. Andreas in his *History of Chicago* published in three volumes between 1884 and 1886 reports that the city's unabashed gaudiness made it a byword for vulgarity and that "Chicago style" in these years became a synonym for bad taste. A major exception was the new Palmer House hotel on State Street designed by Charles M. Palmer under the discerning eye of its owner, Potter Palmer. The Palmer House was inevitably commended for its restrained Parisian elegance.

In the boom decade after the fire, wealthy Chicagoans, who now made it abundantly clear that they did, indeed, know just how rich they were, had no problem finding artistic accoutrements for their houses. Field and Leiter had quickly rebuilt on State Street and in 1882 became Marshall Field's. Judson and Company at the corner of State and Washington streets could make one rest easily on "Turkish spring beds," or on a hair mattress, and could also supply "Curtains of all Kinds." The Ritchie Carpet Company at the corner of State and Adams streets had the latest fashions in floor covers and also "H. M. Jordan, late with W. and J. Sloane, New York." just in case the prospective buyer wanted advice on Axminster patterns. For that final touch there was always J. J. West's Art Emporium on Wabash Avenue where ladies and gentlemen could find the celebrated Rogers' groups with themes such as "Checkers up at the farm," as well as English parian statuary. Among the most successful Chicago decorators of the era was William Henry Connor who had begun his career embellishing the interiors of Pullman cars. Connor might very well have been responsible for the one that carried Frank Cowperwood from Philadelphia to Chicago in Theodore Dreiser's novel *The Titan:*

> Chicago, when it finally dawned on him, came with a rush on the second morning. He had spent two nights in the gaudy Pullman then provided—a car intended to make up for some of the inconveniences of its arrangements by an over-elaboration of plush and tortured glass.

Perhaps George Pullman had known what he was doing after all when he went to Boston for a decorator.

By the 1880s the interiors of Chicago's mansions were often truly staggering. *Artistic Houses*, a series which describes in detail various American palaces, was published at this time and one of the palaces included was that of coffee and tea importer John W. Doane at 1827 Prairie Avenue.

The vestibule is paved with variegated marbles, and the same material is contained in the wainscoting. Heavy oaken doors, with brilliant-hued stained-glass windows, from Lafarge's [sic] workshop, admit the visitor to a broad hallway leading into the grand or main hall. The large window, luminous with variegated colors as the setting sun kisses its surface with a fond good-night, is of home design, as are also the tall windows on the stair-landings. In this entrance-hall bronze medallions are set into the side-walls, which are covered with a peculiar metallic and ornamented material, and bordered with Lincrusta Walton, now becoming popular. A huge ebony card-receiver turns on a pedestal near the window, and facing the visitor is a fountain, about which are clustered flowers, ferns, and rarer plants.

Let it be quickly said that this was by no means the most elaborate room in Mr. Doane's house, though it was certainly one of the more interesting, and Mr. Doane's house was by no means the most elaborate in Chicago. That accolade most likely would have gone to the Henry J. Willing mansion at the northwest corner of Rush and Ontario streets. A pink limestone Gothic confection, it had one fireplace decorated with figures carved by F. Almenroeder representing Rebecca at the well, Oliver Cromwell, and Moses. Just to make certain that it did not appear unadorned, the fireplace also proudly bore the coats of arms of the major nations of the world.

The mention that the Doane house contained windows by the New York painter John La Farge signifies the fact that in most instances the really important Chicago commissions went to New York decorators. When Cudell and Blumenthal completed Cyrus McCormick's Louvre-like abode at 675 Rush Street in 1879, the interiors were under the direction of the fashionable New York firm of L. Marcott and Company. Apparently taking McCormick's title of "the reaper king" seriously, Marcott frescoed the entrance hall in the style of Henry IV of France and hung the walls of the dining room with rare tapestries that did, indeed, date from Henry's time. To make absolutely certain that no one forgot what had put the food on the table, the dining room's ceiling was painted with images of sheaves of grain and reapers.

The heady mélange of materials in the Doane house, the variegated marbles and stained-glass, the tiles and rare wood, reflect the influence of the preeminent New York decorator of the last quarter of the century, Louis C. Tiffany, who was to play a part in the creation of two of Chicago's outstanding Victorian interiors. Tiffany, who is generally remembered today for his glass, also designed and manufactured furniture, silver, fabrics, and pottery and decorated rooms and entire houses. He loved irregularly shaped interiors, worked with surprising

colors, sought to produce a sense of mystery, and strove for exotic effects. The article on him in *Artistic Houses* reports that in one of his rooms he heightened the impression made by a fireplace "by covering the wall just above it with many sheets of mica, through which the light from the fire glistens."

A prime ingredient in all of Louis Tiffany's decoration was the styles of the past—classical, Romanesque, medieval, near eastern. This interest was not original with him, for in 1872 there had appeared the first American edition of *Hints on Household Taste* by the Englishman Charles Eastlake. This book, which called for renewed study of the furniture of earlier periods, had an immediate and telling impact on Americans and many of Louis Tiffany's decorative concepts may be traced to it. Tiffany never slavishly copied past styles, but summoned them up as a base upon which to create something that at once recalled their existence and was, at the same time, very up-to-date, very nineteenth century. In the two most important Chicago interiors in which he had a hand this was most certainly true. For the Pompeiian Room in Holabird and Roche's Congress Hotel of 1893, Tiffany fabricated a tiered blue-green Favrile glass fountain based on his conception of the appearance of ancient Roman glass; and for Shepley, Rutan, and Coolidge's Chicago Public Library of 1897, he supplied the materials for the mosaics which his former colleague, J. A. Holzer, designed in a Byzantine-revival style.

It was inevitable that Chicago's most notable late nineteenth-century residence, that of Potter Palmer on Lake Shore Drive, should have been decorated by yet another fashionable New York firm and that its decor should have borne the unmistakable imprint of Charles Eastlake. The Palmer mansion's exterior was designed in 1882 by Cobb and Frost in a manner deemed to be "castellated Gothic" but which wags said resembled no castle but the one in a fishbowl. Its interiors were constructed by yet two other architects, Silsbee and Kent, while the contracting decorators were Herter Brothers who, like Tiffany, designed and manufactured furniture. The sumptuous rooms that Gustave and Christian Herter assembled of ideas snatched from places as diverse as the Indies, Constantinople, and Araby were among the more awesome sights of late Victorian Chicago and were aptly characterized by Henry B. Fuller in his novel *With the Procession* as "an exhibition of decorative whip-cracking." Mrs. Palmer filled the rooms with precious objects purchased from her favorite Chicago art dealer, Benjamin K. Smith, with rare medieval bibleots from the Paris dealer Raoul Heilbronner, and with magnificent paintings, the now-famed Impressionist ones coming from the great Parisian gallery of Durand-Ruel.

The Palmer castle, with its exteriors designed by one set of architects, its interiors by another, and its decoration in the hands of still other men, is a kind of symbol. It marks just how far things had moved in the century since Robert Adam and William Kent had charge of every detail of the houses they designed. There certainly was no connection between the appearance of the exterior of the Palmers' Rhenish retreat and the chambers within. Indeed, one of them, the twenty-two- by forty-four-foot drawing room had originally been decorated in 1885 by the Herters in an East Indian mode with its intricately carved teakwood walls and ceiling brought from India. Within two years Mrs. Palmer found the room too solemn and had the Herters re-do it in a shimmering Louis XV style that more closely matched the spirit of the Gilded Age.

Yet change was in the air. Within a year of the completion of the Palmer mansion a commission was given to raise a structure in the heart of Chicago which would exhibit once again an architect assuming control over the myriad details of design connected with a huge project. When Ferdinand Peck chose Dankmar Adler and Louis Sullivan to design and construct the Auditorium block with its complex combination of hotel, offices, and opera house, he expected a good building, what he got was a revolutionary one. The engineering genius involved was Dankmar Adler, who had helped to construct bridges for General William Tecumseh Sherman on his march from Atlanta to the sea; the design genius was Louis Sullivan. No detail was too insignificant to escape Sullivan's attention, whether it was the pattern of the fabric on a chair or that of the mosaic floor which, with a *fleur-de-lis,* quietly expressed the indelible impression the stones of Florence had made upon him. To see Sullivan's inexhaustibly inventive drawings for the plaster settings of the Auditorium theatre's carbon filament lights is to know that an earlier, a pre-nineteenth-century spirit of architecture has returned. Sullivan, of course, had assistants—the painters Thomas Healy and Louis Millet, and young draftsmen including George Grant Elmslie and Frank Lloyd Wright—but their role, at most, was akin to that of Thomas Chippendale carrying out the conceptions of Robert Adam.

Sullivan's one hero among the American architects of his day, Henry Hobson Richardson, had begun, in structures such as Boston's Trinity Church, to reclaim for the architect the power to be master of all he built. Richardson, unfortunately, was to die at the comparatively early age of forty-seven with his mission incomplete, while Sullivan would live on into his late sixties. Though the lambent Chicago rooms—the Auditorium Theatre, McVicker's, the trading hall of the Stock Exchange—which show him at his most creative were all built before 1900, he would use his bitter, late years to write those querulous but penetrating books such as the *Kindergarten Chats* with its dismissal of Bradford Gilbert's Illinois Central Depot as having been designed in "the public-be-damned style" and Daniel Burnham's Marshall Field's men's store as a building "made up of particles." Through his writings as well as his structures Sullivan would ultimately help focus attention on the importance of the architect being in charge of all aspects of his buildings. That is the meaning of the historic declaration in the *Chats:*

"The architecture we see today has lost its organic quality."

Sullivan's was not the only voice denouncing the architecture of "particles." In England, the poet, visionary, designer, and architect, William Morris, had been saying much the same thing. In a speech delivered in 1878 under the title "The Decorative Arts: Their Relation to Life and Progress" Morris warned: "I must in plain words say of the Decorative Arts . . . that they are in a state of anarchy and disorganization." The reason, Morris observed, sounding not unlike Louis Sullivan, was that architecture, sculpture, and painting "have fallen apart from one another." Morris thought that they could be put back together again if society would return to the time of the craftsman when every object was beautiful because it had been made by the hand of man. This became the great theme of the arts and crafts movement which Morris founded. The enemy was the Industrial Revolution which had inundated the earth with its effluvium of machine-made, mass-produced goods. To help achieve his goals Morris set up a decorating firm, eventually called Morris and Company, which produced furniture, fabrics, and wallpapers for the dwellings being built by arts and crafts inspired architects like Philip Webb. These designs began turning up with some frequency in Chicago houses well before the turn-of-the-century. In a late nineteenth-century album of photographs of the William O. Goodman residence on Greenwood Avenue, for instance, a Morris-type chair, surprisingly, refreshingly, suddenly appears in a bedroom while all the other rooms are chocked with a too rich array of elaborately carved furniture.

In 1897 two more voices, one of them a woman's, joined the growing chorus of those demanding that the decoration and architecture of a structure be considered together. The woman, Edith Wharton, had already published a few short stories and poems, but the novel *The House of Mirth,* which was to make her reputation, would not appear for another eight years. In 1893 she and her husband Teddy had bought a rather ugly cottage, "Land's End" in Newport, Rhode Island, and found, in Mrs. Wharton's words, "a clever young Boston architect, Ogden Codman" to put it in order for them. "Ogden Codman," writes Florence Codman in her fascinating monograph entitled *The Clever Young Boston Architect,* "had already drawn up the plans and done the interior decoration of houses in Boston, New York, and Newport . . . he had developed from further experience some very positive aesthetic ideas, one of the firmest being that, in contrast to contemporary architectural practice, domestic buildings and their furnishings should be the work of the same designer." Codman would later be commissioned to carry out important decorating projects for Cornelius Vanderbilt at "The Breakers" in Newport and for John D. Rockefeller at "Kyhuit" in Tarrytown, New York.

Mrs. Wharton not only liked the work Codman did for her at "Land's End," she liked his ideas as well. She herself was to characterize most decorating as then practiced as "a branch of dress-making." Eventually Codman and Wharton decided to write a book on the subject and, when *The Decoration of Houses* appeared, it is not surprising that it announced in the introduction that it would treat *"house-decoration as a branch of architecture."*

The idea could scarcely be called new. It would not have been new to Louis Sullivan or to McKim, Mead, and White who in 1892 on Bellevue Place had built a fine Georgian house for Byran Lathrop. It most certainly would not have been new to Richard Morris Hunt who in 1884 had constructed a fairy-tale French Chateau for William Borden on Lake Shore Drive. Nor would it have been a new idea to those august French decorators with their roots in the eighteenth century, Allard et Fils—later to join with Alavoine et Cie—who had, by the 1880s, set up a branch in New York. What was unprecedented about *The Decoration of Houses* was that it had been written by Americans and that it collected between the covers of a single book a wide, almost complete range of decorative problems—walls, windows, fireplaces, and the like—and supported the authors' solutions to those problems with well-reasoned theories.

The volume has few kind things to say about English or American taste:

> English taste has never been so sure as that of the Latin races; and it has, moreover, been perpetually modified by a passion for contriving all kinds of supposed 'conveniences,' which instead of simplifying life not infrequently tend to complicate it. Americans have inherited this trait, and in both countries the architect and upholsterer who can present a new and more intricate way of planning a house or of making a piece of furniture is more sure of a hearing than he who follows the accepted lines.

One thinks immediately of that huge ebony card-receiver turning on its pedestal in John W. Doane's Prairie Avenue mansion.

Though Codman and Wharton have many complimentary things to say about Italian architecture and decoration, the "accepted lines" in their book are usually those of seventeenth- and eighteenth-century France. Eastlake is beyond the pale and so too is Robert Adam, while the flower-patterned wallpapers William Morris designed with such care are condemned not only for being ugly, but unhealthy.

Beneath *The Decoration of Houses* somewhat supercilious surface there lies a wealth of good sense. It wittily attacks the vogue for enormous sliding doors that are never closed and thus destroy all privacy in a house; it ridicules the vast formal salon which seems empty unless a grand ball is in progress; it warns against the Victorian fabric-festooned mantel as a fire hazard. Most importantly, the book makes the point time and again that most so-called decoration is necessary because of defects in the architecture of interiors, that it is, in fact, a mere slip cover over a deformed structure. "Lingerie effects do not combine well with architecture," the authors observe, "and the more architecturally a window is treated, the less it needs to be dressed in ruffles." After *The Decoration of Houses* it became difficult not to think of decoration as a branch of architecture.

Codman and Wharton's aesthetic concepts found their ultimate fulfillment in the work of the Ecole-des-Beaux-Arts-educated Chicago architect, David Adler. With interiors, such as the circular dining room of the Louis XVI style townhouse he designed for Joseph T. Ryerson in 1921 on Astor Street, Adler proved that, indeed, a house possessed with good interior architecture needs very little of what had been thought of as decoration. In addition, the chamber's splendid boiseries, its mirrors, and mantelpiece, all executed in a faultless Louis XVI manner, both reflect the residence's exterior and reveal an architect in full charge of his building.

Some have condemned this type of architecture as mere copying. Louis Sullivan, seeking an all-new American architecture, most certainly looked balefully upon David Adler's houses and would have quoted, if he had quoted anyone but himself, this passage from the architect John Wellborn Root's essay "A Few Practical Hints on Design" written in the early 1890s:

> The temptation is almost irresistible often to take refuge in the books, among the Greeks, among the French; to seek cover in the darkness of the middle ages, or concealment in the glitter of the seventeenth century; to quote precedents, and turn to buildings erected by great men.

But Root, whose final judgments are often more judicious than Sullivan's, whose words are less invective laden, went on in his essay to say that, ultimately, architects must "use all that men have done, to use it all intelligently and consistently, with study and the nicest discrimination, and to make sure that the particular thing chosen for the given purpose shall be the best fitted for that purpose." Adler's reason for selecting the Louis XVI style for his Astor Street townhouse was to provide the Ryersons with an elegant yet restrained ambiance. Unquestionably, the "thing" chosen for that purpose was fitted for the purpose.

If Ogden Codman and Edith Wharton set out to create an aesthetic of decoration, then Elsie de Wolfe, later Lady Mendl, made interior decorating a profession. In the years just before and after the turn-of-the-century, she created a mild sensation because of the manner in which she had fixed up the small house she shared with Elizabeth Marbury on New York's Irving Place. Her "white decor," so named because of her penchant for enamelling dark Victorian furniture white, her use of simple, striped wallpapers, her banishment of bric-a-brac, all led to bright, well-composed interiors that were a breath of fresh air in gloomy brownstone Gotham. Others wanted their houses decorated like hers, and Elsie de Wolfe was, for a price, willing to oblige. Thus she became, for all practical purposes, America's first paid "decorator," as distinguished from nineteenth-century glazers and from designers and manufacturers, such as Tiffany and the Herters, and architects such as Codman. Elsie de Wolfe's big break came in 1905 when, through a friend, Anne Morgan, J. P.'s daughter, she was commissioned to decorate the rooms of the new federal-revival home Stanford White had designed on Madison Avenue for the elite New York woman's club, the Colony. Her enormous success with this project made her not only a paid decorator, but a highly paid one.

Elsie de Wolfe's ideas owe a great deal to Odgen Codman and Edith Wharton. She too found most of her "accepted lines" in France, and like her mentors would eventually settle there. She too preferred architectural rooms and created them when the budgets of her clients permitted. But when the budgets were limited, Elsie de Wolfe was quite ready to create attractive effects with chintz, paint, and pretty pictures. Because of this, Mrs. Wharton would undoubtedly have branded not a little of her work "a branch of dress-making." In 1913 she published *The House in Good Taste,* a book which became a kind of manual for decorators. It lists her likes—small, intimate rooms—and her dislikes—Tiffany lamps, the mention of which resulted in thousands of them landing on the dust heap. It is a book, too, as shown by the following passage, which shares with *The Decoration of Houses* a disdain of pretentious ignorance:

I remember taking a clever Englishwoman of much taste to see a woman who was very proud of her new house. We had seen most of the house when the hostess, who had evidently reserved what she considered the best for the last, threw open the doors of a large and gorgeous apartment and said, "This is my Louis XVI ballroom." My friend, who had been very patient up to that moment, said very quietly, "What makes you think so?"

Elsie de Wolfe not only invented the profession of the paid decorator but by her personal example and by her insouciant remarks, such as "Men are forever guests in our homes," she made it a profession open to women. Her train was composed of famed New York decorators such as Mrs. Henry Parish and Rose Cummings. In Chicago there was Mabel Schamberg, Mildred Newgass, who did apartments in the 1930s in impeccable English style, and Mrs. Clifford Rodman, whose "rooms" at Marshall Field's set a high standard of taste for the entire Midwest in the years just before the Second World War. But Chicago's supreme woman decorator was Rue Winterbotham, Mrs. John Alden Carpenter, who left a lasting remembrance of beauty in the Casino and Fortnightly clubs. The novelist Arthur Meeker hit the mark when he said of her in his memoir, *Chicago with Love:* "She was, I would judge, one of the two most important decorators of the early 1900s in America. At any rate, she was the only one to be mentioned in the same breath with Elsie de Wolfe."

Ogden Codman, Edith Wharton, and David Adler were all, indeed, advocates of a unity, a consistency between a structure's architecture and its interior decoration, but they all found that unity by, in John Wellborn Root's phrase, taking "refuge in the books." Another stream of American decoration had its source in the ideas of William Morris. Though Morris too looked to the past, he turned to it primarily for its ethics rather than its aesthetics. His minimally decorated wooden chairs, the designs of his papers and fabrics, were emphatically not the product of a copyist. One of Morris' greatest American disciples, Gustav Stickley, was by 1900 producing furniture in his Eastwood workshop outside of Syracuse, New York, which was to prove an inspiration to Chicago designers and architects.

The October 1901 issue of *House and Garden* magazine carries on its editorial page a most interesting statement:

Few architects have sufficient fertility and versatility to design the entire setting of the life that is to go on within their houses. In our country there comes to mind no one but Frank Lloyd Wright.

Wright, the outstanding member of the Prairie School, is also the outstanding example of the influence of William Morris' arts and crafts ideals upon Chicago architects. Though it is impossible to deny Wright's own creative genius, it is also true, as David Hanks points out in *The Decorative Designs of Frank Lloyd Wright,* that Wright sometimes used Stickley's furniture in his houses when his clients could not afford to have the architect design the pieces himself, and that Wright knew of and admired the work of the Morris-inspired Scotch designer Charles Rennie Mackintosh. The influence of Morris is evident in Wright's uncompromisingly straight-backed unpainted chairs, in his fascination with art-glass, and in his built-in furniture. All of these he designed with equal facility for Frank Lloyd Wright reaches back through Sullivan to the concept of the architect as the complete draftsman. In structures, such as his own residence and studio of 1889-95 and in the Unity Church of 1906, both in Oak Park, and in the luminiscent bookstore he designed in the Fine Arts Building in 1908, Wright gave ample proof that he could not conceive of decoration other than as a branch of architecture and that he had the "fertility and versatility to design the entire setting."

But Wright was not the only Chicago architect in 1901 with such powers. If *House and Garden* had done its homework, it would have added to its list the name of another arts and crafts disciple, George W. Maher, who, in his massive James A. Patten house built that very year in Evanston, took charge of the design of the woodwork, fireplaces, glass, and much of the furniture. It would also have added the talented George Grant Elmslie who could design a perfect side chair as well as an entire building. In 1912, working closely with the decorator and furniture maker George Niedecken, Elmslie would produce in the Edison Phonograph Shop on Wabash Avenue interiors that were a triumphant interpretation of the ideals of the arts and crafts movement and a structure whose exterior and interior were parts of a perfect whole.

It is against this background that the appearance in Chicago in the late 1930s of the Bauhaus refugee designers and architects, particularly Mies van der Rohe, must be viewed. In an essay in 1923, "The Theory and the Organization of the Bauhaus," its founder, the architect Walter Gropius, had announced, "We want to create a clear, organic architecture, whose inner logic will be radiant and naked, unencumbered by lying facades and trickeries." Gropius also called for painting, sculpture, graphics, and architecture to work together, not to pull apart from one another. The words and the thoughts echo Morris and Sullivan and even, curiously, Codman and Wharton. Today they do not sound as startling as they did when Mies and Gropius were alive to stentorianly reiterate them.

Mies did, indeed, in his 860-880 Lake Shore Drive Apartments of 1952 carry the concept of naked architecture to its logical conclusion. In so doing, he also pushed to its extreme the idea of the architect in control of the interiors of his structure, for in these sophisticated glass and steel towers there is scarcely any visible barrier between outside and inside. The tenants of the apartments are permitted but one color and style of drapery, for that which gives color to the rooms also gives color and, to some degree, texture to the buildings' transparent walls. Yet even the aesthetic concept of Mies' Lake Shore Drive Apartments was not entirely new. As Stuart E. Cohen noted in *Chicago Architects* of 1976, with his Crystal House of 1934 built for the Century of Progress Exposition George Fred Keck had constructed the first dwelling in America whose exterior walls were made entirely of glass. Keck, having used the technology of the machine age to, as it were, dissolve the Crystal House's facades, then boldly displayed within it the bright symbols of the new age: chrome and leather furniture and Buckminster Fuller's Dymaxion Car.

By the 1960s, it would have seemed that, for important structures at least, the concept of decoration as a branch of architecture had triumphed. But life and taste are never static. In the mid-1970s, there rose within view of Mies van der Rohe's Lake Shore Drive Apartments the marble-clad hulk of Water Tower Place. The lobby of the complex's Ritz-Carlton Hotel comes as something of a surprise. It is topped by a gold leaf ceiling of intricate and exotic design and has for its centerpiece a fountain in which sport gilded cranes. It is clear that once more the upholsterer has tiptoed in. Those cranes would have delighted John W. Doane and even George M. Pullman might have accepted the burnished birds, that is, if A. H. Davenport had told him exactly where to put them.

DAVID LOWE CHICAGO INTERIORS

One of the prime functions of American hotels has been to provide an escape from the ordinary routine of life. They are, like ocean liners, machines to free their occupants from all domestic responsibility. Hotel interiors aided psychologically in this by providing settings which attempted to carry one away to the courts of European kings, or to castles in Spain, or to ancient Roman cities. A preeminent example of this was the Japanese Tea Room in the Congress Hotel of 1893. Its conception was much influenced by the Japanese tea houses, built by workmen sent from Japan by the Mikado, which represented the Imperial Japanese Government at the Columbian Exposition held in Chicago the same year the Congress opened. Designed by Holabird and Roche, the architects of the hotel, the room was decorated by the painter Edward J. Holslag. Japanese waiters helped provide a sense of authenticity to this masterful invocation of the Land of the Rising Sun. The room was destroyed in the 1930s when the hotel management considered it passé.

I
HOTEL
LIFE

"Me and father have a nice little room to ourselves," the young Willie Lincoln wrote home to a friend in Springfield during a visit he and Abraham Lincoln made to Chicago in June of 1859. The "nice little room" was most likely in the nine-year-old Tremont House at Lake and Dearborn streets, designed by John Van Osdel. The Tremont inaugurated a competition for grandeur among Chicago hotels which has continued for 130 years. It had not only nice little private rooms, but big public ones as well, for *The Illinois State Journal* reported on December 10, 1856 that three hundred Republicans had sat down there to a banquet where: "Every luxury which the fastidious palate could desire . . . was present in bounteous profusion and enjoyed with peculiar unction." Providing luxury and a bit of soothing unction has also been a tradition taken seriously by Chicago hotels.

The Great Fire of 1871 gave Chicago an unparalleled opportunity to build new hotels from the ground up and by 1873 it boasted twenty first-class ones, more than any other city in the country. To turn the pages of an old guide, such as the one John J. Flinn compiled in 1892 for visitors, to "Chicago: The Marvelous City of the West," is to long for a time machine to carry one back to the day when it was possible to see the Auditorium Hotel in its full glory; stroll through the august Grand Pacific where so much of the intrigue of Frank Norris' *The Pit* took place; dine at the aristocratic Leland, later the Stratford; and witness the crowd assembled under the post-fire Palmer House's thirty-six-foot-high rotunda.

The Palmer House was always an object of comment by foreigners. Sir Rose Lambart Price, an English baronet who stayed there in November of 1875, was enthusiastic: "We put up at the Palmer House Hotel, Chicago, Ill., without any exception the finest, best conducted hotel in America." In 1889 Rudyard Kipling enthused a good deal less: "They told me to go to the Palmer House which is a gilded and mirrored rabbit warren, and where I found a huge hall of tessellated marble, crammed with people talking about money . . . ."

Talking about money never embarrassed Chicagoans; they were well aware that money was behind all that tessellated marble. But then the English always made the Windy City uneasy. In the 1870s, when the better hotels began offering guests the choice of either the American plan (room and board) or the European plan (a room without meals), a visiting Britisher was asked by a Palmer House clerk, "American or European?" The answer came back briskly, "English."

The Great Row

The opening in 1889 of Dankmar Adler and Louis Sullivan's Auditorium Hotel, seen at left in this 1890 view up Michigan Avenue, marked the beginning of the avenue's great hotel row. Though the street had boasted fine hostelries before this, Sullivan and Adler's 400-room behemoth, part of a complex that included an opera house, restaurants, and commercial offices, introduced them on a new, monumental scale. Through the 1930s, one could dine on the open-air balcony above the hotel's main entrance. It was on this balcony in June of 1892 that Theodore Dreiser, as a young reporter for the Chicago *Daily Globe,* got the scoop that Grover Cleveland was to be the Democratic nominee which launched his career. "Here I sat on this grand balcony . . . the lovely panorama of the lake and Michigan Drive below."—Theodore Dreiser, *A Book About Myself.*

One of the most notable rooms in the Auditorium was the banquet hall (above), daringly suspended on 118-foot-long bridgelike trusses over the opera house. While Sullivan himself supervised every detail of this room, the elaborately carved birch capitals of the columns were executed by R. W. Bates and the frescoes and other decoration by Thomas Healy and Louis Millet, two of Sullivan's close friends. In the days when formal attire was *de rigueur,* as it was in this 1905 photograph of the annual Chicago Jewelers Association banquet, the room's sumptuous decor complemented perfectly its occupants' dress. It now serves as a recital hall for Roosevelt University.

*Right:*A menu for a card club dinner at the Auditorium Hotel, with dishes named after club members. Skat, from which the club derived its name, was a three-hand game played with 32 cards and was very popular with gentlemen in the 1890s.

MENU

SOLO BLUE POINTS

CONSOMME NUL OVERT

SMALL PATTIES, A LA SADOWITZ

BLACK BASS A LA CARL GODFRIED, GUCKSE-GRANDO
POTATOES ?   CUCUMBERS TURNTERT

BREAST OF CHICKEN, A LA LEHMAN MAURER

PUNCH GRAND OHNE VIEREN, A LA HOTZ

ROAST QUAIL, STUFFED, A LA REHM
SALAD: SPIELT-ABER-NIE

FANCY ICE CREAM, RAMSCH

CAKES HERZ   CHEESE ANGESAGT

CAFE SCHWARTZ

LIEBFRAUMILCH   PONTET CANET   CLICQUOT, YELLOW LABEL

THE THURSDAY EVENING SKAT CLUB.
AUDITORIUM HOTEL.
NOV. 9, 1898.

Among the best of the pre-Auditorium hotels of Michigan Avenue was the Stratford on the near right in this 1913 view looking south from the Art Institute. Designed by William W. Boyington, the hotel began life in 1872 as the Gardner House, was re-christened the Leland in 1881 and got its final name at the turn-of-the-century. In the 1900 photograph of its lobby corridor (right), Boyington's original vocabulary of classical moldings and columns has been updated by the addition of 1890s arts and crafts woodwork and stained glass. The most famous of all Chicago hotel corridors was Peacock Alley (right below) in Holabird and Roche's 1,200-room Congress. Built in four sections, the oldest section of the Congress opened in 1893 for the Columbian Exposition as the Annex. The gleaming white marble "Alley" connected the main lobby with the Elizabethan Room and was Chicago's answer to a similarly named "Alley" Henry J. Hardenbergh had created in New York's Waldorf Hotel. It was up this corridor in 1912 that Theodore Roosevelt strode to open his Bull Moose convention in the Auditorium, and it was here that Franklin D. Roosevelt, after winning the Democratic nomination for

President in 1932, first heard "Happy Days Are Here Again."

In one of the worst acts of vandalism perpetrated against any surviving Chicago structure, after the Second World War Peacock Alley was redesigned in a characterless, commercial "modern" style.

Few hotels in the world could match the variety of superbly decorated rooms contained within Holabird and Roche's Congress, (whose ground floor plan is seen at right). The Gold Room (above), while officially labeled as Louis XV, was in reality one of the world's most magnificent Second Empire spaces with the plaster musical figures above the arches consciously recalling the work of Jean Baptiste Carpeaux at the Paris Opera. The decoration of the Gold Room, a favorite locale for society balls in the Gilded Decades, was carried out by Edward J. Holslag, a pupil of the

painter John La Farge. Holslag also did the murals for the Pompeiian Room (left) with its furniture from Marshall Field and Company and its 8-foot-high urns made by the American Terra Cotta Company. The tiered fountain of blue-green glass which graced the center court was the work of Louis C. Tiffany. A remark by the social critic and wit, H. L. Mencken, made the room famous. "Chicago," Mencken quipped, "has just two things New York doesn't; the Pompeiian Room and the Twentieth Century Limited back to New York."

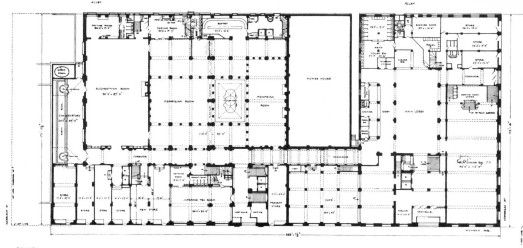

In 1910 the social supremacy of the Congress Hotel was challenged by Marshall and Fox's Blackstone, located a block farther south on Michigan at what is now Balbo Avenue. The interiors of the 500-room hotel were the work of Benjamin H. Marshall and show the influence of London's Ritz Hotel, completed four years earlier. The restaurant (above) in soft pearl gray and the ballroom in white and gold were Chicago's best examples of the opulent, Edwardian Beaux-Arts style. The Blackstone became the stopping off place for every President from Theodore Roosevelt to Richard M. Nixon.

Still farther south at the southwest corner of Michigan and Balbo avenues, the Great Row reached a climax with the 1927 opening of Holabird and Roche's 3,000-room Stevens. Working closely with the hotel's owner, Ernest J. Stevens, decorator Norman Tolson produced what the June 1927 issue of *Good Furniture* magazine called an interior "Rich and costly, but of a dignified simplicity" which ran the gamut of styles from Louis XIV through Directoire to Empire. The vast, white marble lobby (right) was crowned with a carved plaster ceiling stained to resemble wood, trimmed in gold, and centered with a painting of clouds by W. P. Nelson. Meyer Levin in *The Old Bunch* remarked on the hotel's size: "The new Stevens Hotel, bigger than the Palmer House, the biggest hotel in the world. Three thousand rooms. You could sleep in a different room every night, till 1935, without duplicating."

In 1951 the Stevens was renamed the Conrad Hilton.

Magnificence in the Loop

In the middle of the nineteenth century, the combination of the Erie, Illinois, and Michigan canals and an expanding railroad network made Chicago the crossroads of the nation. The city then began constructing hotels of a splendor which attracted world-wide notice. The site of these hotels was almost inevitably in the heart of the metropolis, that section which became known as the Loop. Here the visitor was close to the financial establishments of La Salle Street, the theatres of Randolph Street, and the tempting bazaars of State Street.

The undoubted queen of the Loop hotels was the Palmer House, which opened in 1873 at State and Monroe streets, succeeding a hotel of that name which was destroyed in the Great Fire of 1871. Designed by Charles Maldon Palmer, the 700-room palace's construction was meticulously supervised by its owner, the merchant and real estate entrepreneur, Potter Palmer. After examining the leading hotels of Europe—the Hotel du Louvre in Paris, Langham's in London, and the Beau Rivage in Geneva—Palmer combined thirty-four varieties of marble, Florentine mosaic mirrors, satin and velvet upholstery, and specially woven Axminster carpets to create an atmosphere which a hotel brochure proclaimed "reminds one of the state apartments of the Tuillieries in the palmy days of the Empire." This hotel was demolished in stages between 1923 and 1925.

Potter Palmer, as the announcement above plainly shows, was a man who knew the value of a dollar or a gold piece. He once forced several guests who owed him money to stand in the lobby with signs which read "Hotel Deadbeat." The check-in lobby (below) had counters of white carrara marble set with panels of rose, while the columns with gilded capitals were of yellow brocatelle marble veined with red from Catalonia.

The hallway on the second floor of the Palmer House (above) was furnished with chandeliers and candelabra from France. The doors at the far end of the hall lead to the bridal chamber. The well-organized kitchen (right) reflects Palmer's love of good food. It was situated in a separate building erected in a courtyard so that cooking odors would not enter the hotel, and was supplied with water from a private artesian well.

The first half of the third Palmer House opened in 1926 and, by the time the second half opened in 1927, its twenty-four floors held 2,250 rooms and had cost more than $20,000,000. The hotel was the work of Holabird and Roche, whose interior design department with direction from John Wellborn Root, Jr., chose a crisp, modified First Empire style for most of the structure's public rooms. The Great Hall, or lobby (above), was given warmth by its Roman travertine walls, its velvet upholstered furniture supplied by Carson, Pirie, Scott, and Co., and its colorful classical ceiling (center top) painted by an Italian artisan. The lobby, though marred by the intrusion of two escalators and by modern furniture, is still impressive.

The Empire Room (left), originally the main dining room, became a supper club in 1933. Here a rich contrast was created by placing flat ebony pilasters against dark green walls, with gold leaf used to pick out capitals, cornice, and trim. After years as one of the late-night showplaces of the Loop, featuring stars of the magnitude of Maurice Chevalier, Ethel Merman, Sophie Tucker, and Louis Armstrong, the Empire Room ceased to be a supper club in January of 1976. The entrance hall of the Ballroom (above), a stately ensemble of Ionic columns supporting a shallow saucer dome, was one of the most elegant spaces ever created in an American hotel. It has, alas, been remodeled beyond recognition.

The chief challenger to the Palmer House's supremacy in the Loop in the last quarter of the nineteenth century was the Grand Pacific Hotel, a mansard-roofed Second Empire extravaganza whose plans and lobby arcade are shown at right. Standing in the block bounded by Clark, Jackson, La Salle, and Quincy streets, it had just been completed when the Great Fire of 1871 gutted it. The Grand Pacific was quickly rebuilt from the original designs of William W. Boyington, Chicago's premier hotel architect who already had more than twenty, including the Sherman House, to his credit. The hotel opened in June 1873 with 200 rooms, though it was eventually to expand to some 900. The Grand Pacific's glass-domed carriage rotunda with direct access to the office rotunda was a welcome innovation in snow-plagued Chicago. Another much-commented-upon innovation was the construction of servants' dormitories in the attic story which prevented them from having to sleep on cots set up each night in the parlors and dining rooms as was the custom.

Spending nearly a half million dollars on furnishings, the Grand Pacific management dressed its public rooms in a variety of styles staggering even by Victorian Chicago standards and offered, among others, an India Room, an Egyptian Room, and an Oriental Parlor for ladies. The bar (far right) had a barrel-vaulted ceiling of Honduras mahogany supported by octagonal columns of deep red and saffron yellow marble, and walls of green damask. Favored for club gatherings (below), the caravansary was famed for its annual invitation-only game dinners whose social importance is

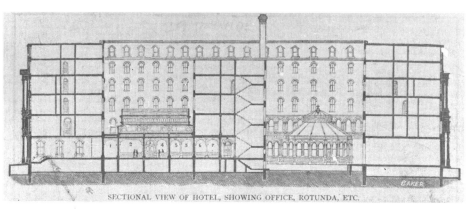

SECTIONAL VIEW OF HOTEL, SHOWING OFFICE, ROTUNDA, ETC.

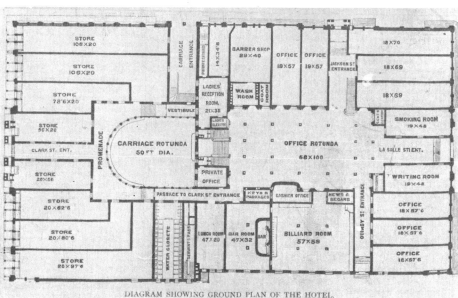

DIAGRAM SHOWING GROUND PLAN OF THE HOTEL.

THE

CHICAGO YALE ASSOCIATION

TWENTY-FOURTH ANNUAL DINNER

DECEMBER 27, 1889,

THE GRAND PACIFIC HOTEL.

noted in Henry B. Fuller's incisive novel of 1890s Chicago, *With the Procession:* "'H'm,' she observed, presently, 'those game-dinners at the Pacific are still going on, aren't they? To-night's the thirty-eighth.'" In the era when Chicago was the world's chief purveyor of game the dinners mustered such arcane delicacies as smoke-cured bear ham and sandhill crane.

The hotel's proximity to the Grain Exchange made it a favorite of La Salle Street traders. For years, as a kind of *momento mori,* the English Room retained the telephone used in 1897-98 by Joseph Leiter, son of merchant Levi Leiter, to buy nearly eighty million bushels of grain in his unsuccessful bid to corner the wheat market. It was also at the Grand Pacific on May 19, 1875 that Mary Todd Lincoln was arrested and declared insane. The historic hotel, whose exterior is seen at right, closed in 1919.

The demand for a new hotel in the financial district led to the opening in 1909 of yet another Holabird and Roche masterpiece, the La Salle, situated on the northwest corner of La Salle and Madison streets. The main entrance is on the near left in this view up La Salle Street through the temporary arch erected for the Grand Encampment of the Knights Templar in August of 1910.

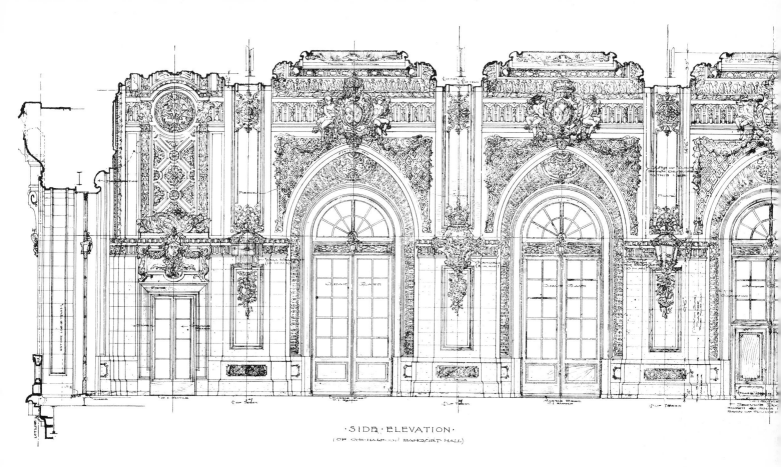

·SIDE·ELEVATION·
(OF ONE-HALF OF BANQUET HALL)

The style of the hotel was a mixture of Louis XIV and Louis XV. The dark French Circassian walnut paneling of the lobby (left above) by the Chicago firm of Hilger and Co. was, in the words of the architect, Martin Roche, supposed to "have a distinctly homelike feeling." The ballroom (below) on the nineteenth floor measured an imposing 140 feet in length. It was the color of Caen stone with touches of gold, violet, and gray-blue. The fine sculpture work, a detail of which is shown in the drawing above, was by another Chicago firm, Beil and Hermant. The La Salle was demolished in 1977.

The hotels north of the Loop, that is north of the Chicago River, were originally built to cater primarily to permanent residents. The pioneering structure here was the 500-room Edgewater Beach, which was located on the lake at 5300 North Sheridan Road and opened in 1916. Designed throughout by Benjamin H. Marshall of the firm of Marshall and Fox, the hotel's yellow stucco exterior struck a note that was carried out in its Mediterranean interiors of cast concrete. At left is the hotel's splendid lobby before its great free-standing fireplace was removed in the 1930s and below is the Edgewater's private omnibus. The Edgewater Beach was demolished in 1969.

The Pearson Hotel at 190 East Pearson Street was Chicago's preeminent Georgian-style hostelry. When it opened in 1923 its fourteen-story refined red brick and limestone facade fit perfectly into the almost Bostonian reserve of Streeterville, as the district between North Michigan Avenue and the lake was then popularly called. Its architect, Robert S. De Golyer, gave the hotel a series of brilliant interiors of understated splendor such as the Dining Room shown above. De Golyer, who is now almost forgotten, was an architect with a profound knowledge of the historic styles. He was responsible for a number of luxury apartment buildings that went up in Chicago in the 1920s, including the Barry Apartments, the Marlborough, and 1120 Lake Shore Drive, as well as the vanished Italian Court on Michigan Avenue. The Pearson, unfortunately, was leveled in 1972 to make way for the Ritz-Carlton Hotel.

Chicago hotels were always considered appropriate residences for visiting dignitaries. During his 1860 stopover, the Prince of Wales, later Edward VII, put up at the Richmond House; and General Ulysses S. Grant never stayed at his in-laws' (the Potter Palmers) castle but at their hotel. During her visit to the city from November 13 to 17, 1926, the dramatic Queen Marie of

Roumania lodged at the fashionable Lake Shore Drive Hotel. Marie's twenty-four-room suite, whose Florentine Salon is shown at top left, was said to include three chairs from the late Czar of Russia's palace and was decorated by William R. Moore. Though it had all the trappings of a set for a Valentino movie, the designer characterized it as "very simple and very American." Far left, below, a maid gives the Queen's bed a final pat.

Near left below is Chicago's own version of royalty, the Countess Cizycka at the Lake Shore Drive Hotel in 1924. The countess was née Eleanor Medill Patterson and was a granddaughter of the founder of the *Chicago Tribune.*

At right is the Plaza Hotel which overlooked Lincoln Park at the corner of Clark Street and North Avenue. It opened in 1892 and survived until the mid-1960s. Designed by Clinton J. Warren, the exterior of the Plaza Hotel combined elevations which were rather powerful examples of the architecture of the first Chicago School topped by a Beaux-Arts cornice. The Plaza's lobby (below) was a delightful Gay Nineties confection of bright gilt, pastel colors, and paintings of spring flowers and Gainsborough-inspired beauties.

II PLAYER WITH RAILROADS

The Midwest and the railroad grew up together. They are both inventions of the nineteenth century. For the states of the Atlantic Coast, romantic travel always meant the sea, first clipper ships and later the great ocean liners; for California and most of the West, transportation meant automobiles and airplanes; for Midwesterners, travel conjured up the image of the railroad. It recurs like an incessant theme of a symphony in the writing of Midwesterners. "Nicole was the product of much ingenuity and toil. For her sake trains began their run in Chicago . . . " F. Scott Fitzgerald wrote in *Tender Is the Night*. Sinclair Lewis in *Main Street* observed: " . . . the train plodded through the gray prairie, on a windless day with the smoke from the engine clinging to the fields like giant cotton-rolls."

Nowhere was the spell of the iron horse more evident than in the metropolis of the Midwest, Chicago. "This great city," William T. Stead noted in *If Christ Came to Chicago!*, "is stretched over a gridiron of rails." It was indeed. At the height of the power of the rails in the early 1920s, Chicago possessed more than one hundred railway yards and forty percent of all the railway mileage in the United States terminated in the Windy City. In 1921, its thirty-nine railroads moved more than 20,000,000 freight cars and almost 70,000,000 passengers through the city. During that year a train arrived in or departed from Chicago every minute of every hour of every day. Carl Sandburg did not exaggerate when he indelibly dubbed Chicago, "Player with Railroads."

Go Pullman

One of Chicago's preeminent trains was the New York Central's Twentieth Century Limited, shown overleaf in Chicago in 1931. In its glamorous days between the two World Wars, the Twentieth Century left the La Salle Street Station each afternoon at 2:00 and reached New York eighteen hours later. Among its luxurious services was direct telephone communication which began twenty minutes before starting time. The Twentieth Century's fabled number was WABash 4200.

It is not surprising that the highest expression of the American railway car should have been a Chicago product. In 1859 George M. Pullman spent $2,000 to remodel a day coach owned by the Chicago and Alton Railroad into a sleeping car. With the help of the skilled woodworker, Leonard Seibert, Pullman created a car with two washrooms, a linen locker, and ten sections that converted into beds. That coach, known as old "No. 9," is shown opposite above.

In 1863 Pullman constructed his first all-new car, the Pioneer, and by 1867 there were forty-eight Pullman cars rolling across the country as proof that passengers were willing to pay an extra two dollars a night for a comfortable bed. Within a very short time, as shown by the 1873 Erie Railway advertisement opposite, the quality of a line's service could be gauged by the number and variety of Pullman cars that it offered its passengers.

Among the many special cars constructed by the Pullman Palace Car Company was a Tabernacle Car (left) which, in addition to the usual sleeping accommodations, carried two organs. It was used on weekend runs between Chicago and the West Coast by the Union Pacific in the 1870s.

Pullman was also famed for its luxurious private cars which were built for both individuals and businesses. The Ely (above) was constructed in the 1880s as a company car. Its very masculine appointments, including the fine walnut desks in its conference room, recreated the atmosphere of a serious office of the day. The Ely was used for a number of years by the Nevada Northern Railroad.

The marked elaboration of interior detail from the first Pullman car of 1859 to cars such as the Ely built in the 1880s was not merely a by-product of the Pullman Company's increasing affluence but was the direct result of its desire to keep the design of its products up-to-date. For the Columbian Exposition held in Chicago in 1893, Pullman created dazzling cars for the Illinois Central's new "Diamond Special." The smoking room was, according to a report of the day, "finished in African vermilion wood of exquisite grain, relieved by embossed gold-leather panels and frieze, with carpeted floor and finely decorated ceiling to match."

By the time the smoking and club car (above) was in use on the Twentieth Century Limited in 1932, Pullman had opted for far more straightforward designs. The car's decoration was confined to a frieze running around the walls and its beamed ceiling. Interestingly, the design is an unmistakable echo of the Congress Hotel's Pompeiian Room, so that

MAIDENLY FEARS.

Miss Prunella Bombazine *(her first sleeping-car experience).*—Are you sure you locked the door, Porter? I thought I heard somebody come in!

the traveler could have that famous chamber and the Twentieth Century all in one.

The Pullman Company consistently stressed the advantages of its modern and clean lavatories, a refreshing novelty on the smoky trains of the nineteenth century. At far left, this woodcut entitled "Morning Ablutions" appeared in *Frank Leslie's Illustrated Newspaper* and pictured the lavatory of the Pullman "Hotel Car" in which Mr. Leslie himself rode from Chicago to the Pacific in the summer of 1877.

Pullman frequently made the point that though there might be physical proximity to other passengers, there was never even a hint of promiscuity. The point is made humorously in this 1888 cartoon (above left); it is made quietly in the 1923 Rock Island advertisement (below left) captioned "Make yourself at home"; and it is made alluringly by the photograph (above) of these 1939 lovelies in their safe and cozy Union Pacific berths.

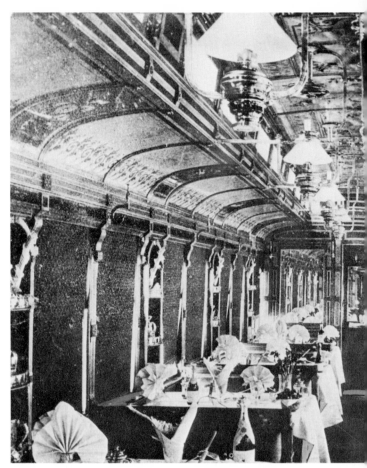

Always alert to new ways to promote his company, in 1867 George Pullman began setting up tables in his "Hotel Cars" and serving meals as shown in the 1873 engraving above. Suddenly it was no longer necessary for hungry travelers to dash out of trains and grab a quick bite at stations. As with almost everything Pullman did, the idea was an immediate success and the company could soon proclaim that its bill of fare "would cause Delmonico to wring his hands in anguish."

By the late 1870s when the Pullman Company was building complete dining cars, some of its specialties had become world-famous, such as the rainbow trout plucked from the icy waters of the Rockies and "The best ham what am" supplied by the pioneering Chicago packing house of Morris and Company. Its menus also offered woodcock and prairie chicken for $1.00 and sirloin steak for 50¢.

One of the first lines to experiment with restaurant cars west of Chicago was the Rock Island. Its "Oriental" (center top) began operating between Chicago and Council Bluffs, Iowa in 1878. (The Rock Island's three other original dining cars were named Occidental, Overland, and Australia.) The sparkling cars made a deep impression on travelers in the heartland. It was just such a car that delighted Thea Kronborg, the heroine of Willa Cather's *Song of the Lark,* when she traveled between Chicago and her home in Moonstone, Colorado: "At that early hour there were few people in the dining-car. The linen was white and fresh . . . and the sunlight gleamed pleasantly upon the silver and the glass water-bottles. On each table there was a slender vase with a single pink rose in it."

28

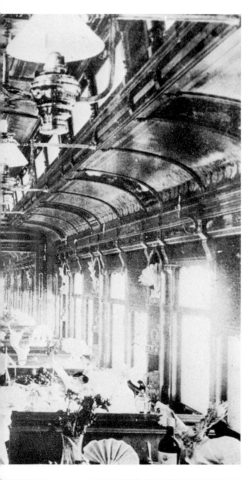

The Twentieth Century, like most crack trains, made a point of keeping its design up-to-the-minute, although the dining car on the first Twentieth Century in 1902 (center bottom) was actually an 1896 design. Gone are the hanging lamps of the "Oriental" and the painted decoration of the ceiling, but the high leather-backed chairs and the bottle glass in the top of the curved windows relate this car to the dark taprooms of the Gilded Age. By the time Henry Dreyfus re-did the Twentieth Century in 1938 (below), all of this had disappeared. Dreyfus, one of the leading industrial designers of the thirties who did much work for the Crane Company, created a sleek streamlined interior which marks the last step in the evolution of the American railway car. The perfection attained in the interior of the Twentieth Century Limited in the late 1930s was matched by its Dreyfus-designed appointments of china, crystal, and Belgium linen. The variety of food offered was equally impressive, with some 300 different items available, including lobsters kept alive in a salt water tank.

From a design point-of-view the most important of Chicago's nineteenth-century railway stations was Grand Central, which opened in 1890 at Harrison Street and Fifth Avenue, later Wells Street. It was the New York railroad magnate Henry Villard who selected the Chicagoan Solon S. Beman (right) as the station's architect. Beman was no novice to the realities of railways, having been the architect of the town George Pullman constructed just south of Chicago in the 1880s for his sleeping car

ne Grand Station

ks and workers.

Grand Central's train shed (left below), its iron and steel plied by the Keystone Bridge npany of Pittsburgh, was a inguished example of Victorian ss and iron architecture. The ting room (below left) continued theme of the curve which man made the essence of the ion's design. It had floors of red white Vermont marble, nscoting of pink Tennessee, and nty-five-foot-high columns of per *faux marbre* made by the Art Marble Company of Chicago.

In its heyday the station was the anchorage of some of the nation's greatest trains such as the Baltimore and Ohio's Number Six to Washington and New York, the Northern Pacific's Pacific Mail to Portland, Oregon, and its Minnesota and Dakota Night Express to Winnepeg. In 1971 Grand Central followed the famous trains it had once sheltered into oblivion.

III ON THE TOWN

In this age when even the smallest hamlet has street lamps and television brings both Hollywood and Broadway into the most isolated home, we have forgotten all that the term "bright lights" connotes. For the Middle West, that vast area between eastern Ohio and western Nebraska where the winters are long and the days often dark and short, "bright lights" meant Chicago. It meant Randolph and State streets, Michigan Avenue and Dearborn; it meant the Windy City's theatres, movie palaces, and dance halls. It was what lured Carrie Meeber, of Theodore Dreiser's *Sister Carrie,* from Wisconsin to Chicago. The bright lights flash on again and again in that profound novel: "They dined and went to the theatre. That spectacle pleased Carrie immensely."

Concert Halls and Theatres

Though Chicago had a theatre tradition stretching back to that day in 1838 when Joseph Jefferson, Sr. appeared in town, the city's contribution to serious theatre architecture began in 1879 with the opening of the 2,000-seat Central Music Hall (below and right). The structure brought together two of Chicago's greatest architects, Dankmar Adler and Louis Sullivan; Adler, who received the commission, hired the younger Sullivan to design the hall's organ grills. The unmistakably ecclesiastical look of the stained glass windows at the rear and of the seats was no accident, for they were specified by one of the hall's chief occupants, the Reverend David Swing. Swing, originally a Presbyterian minister, became a popular independent preacher after being accused of heresy in 1874. The Central Music Hall, which stood on the southeast corner of State and Randolph, disappeared in 1900.

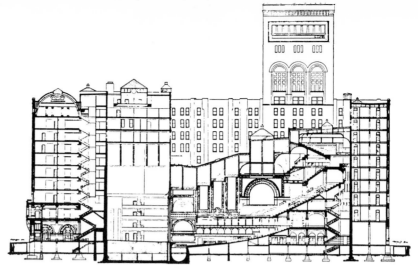

Louis Sullivan set out to invent a new vocabulary of decoration for the 4,237-seat Auditorium Theatre of 1889. (A cross section of the Auditorium building is shown above.) Often he climbed over the scaffolding, shown at right, to supervise the workmen as they put the finishing touches on his wonderful hall. His handiwork was everywhere—in the gilded plaster of the powerful arches, in the patterns of the rugs, in the golden stencils of the stair landings, in the upholstery of the seats, in the stained glass windows of the lobby—all of which he designed. Sometimes, as with the frieze above the boxes (far right above), the inspiration came from Celtic sources; sometimes, as with the arcade framing the boxes, it stems from his love of nature also celebrated in his poetry: "Now am I 'neath the heavy, spreading bough." In the overall scheme there is a certain similarity to Louis Tiffany's design for New York's Lyceum Theatre of 1885. The final result was a glorious house for music and theatre, with acoustics so perfect that Dankmar Adler was to be called to New York to work his magic in Carnegie Hall. It was also a versatile house, one that could either be monumental or, when its ingenius iron panels shut off the two upper galleries and the back of the first balcony, one that could be transformed into a theatre seating just 2,574. The Auditorium's most dramatic moment undoubtedly came in 1910, when a performance of Richard Strauss's *Salome* was closed by the police at the request of the Chicago Law and Order League.

Sullivan's inventive decoration ran into difficulty with the McVicker's Theatre of 1891 (far right). The owner insisted on *bas-relief* panels for both sides of the

stage, one portraying "La Salle's March through Illinois" and the other "The Fort Dearborn Massacre." These were the work of Johannes Gelert. But Sullivan covered the rest of the theatre with the designs that made Frank Lloyd Wright say: "He was miraculous when he drew." These were rendered in ornamental plaster by the firm of Schneider and Kline. McVicker's, on Madison Street just west of State, was replaced by a movie palace of the same name in the 1930s.

The Sullivan and Adler
Auditorium building, with its hotel,
offices, restaurants, and opera
house under one roof, was a
structure which functioned twenty-
four hours a day and was incredibly
efficient in its use of energy. The
opera house itself was
multipurpose. The seats could be
covered by specially designed
planks and the whole theatre could
thus be transformed into a ballroom.
A backdrop used at such times
continued the design of the theatre
in trompe l'oeil. At the height of its
glory at the turn-of-the-century, the
Auditorium was the setting for
elaborate balls (below) given in
honor of visiting dignitaries such as
Prince Henry of Prussia, brother of
Kaiser Wilhelm II. Large dances
were still held in the Auditorium in
the 1930s, as evidenced by this gala
scene of December 22, 1931 (right).
The last days of these big parties
held in the Auditorium Theatre were
in the early 1940s.

In honor of
His Royal Highness
Prince Henry of Prussia
Monday March third 1902
The Auditorium
Chicago

36

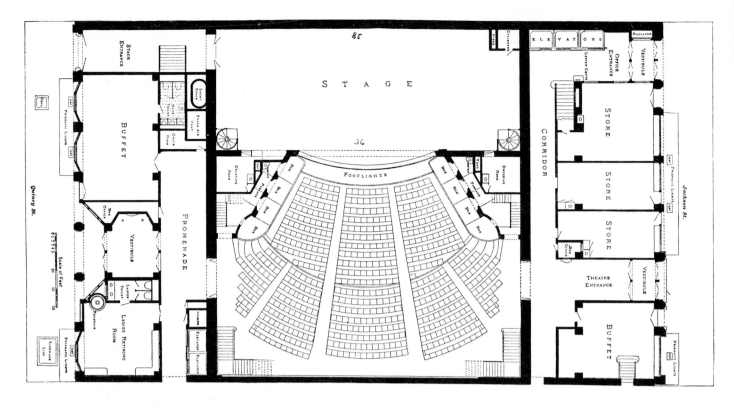

Louis Sullivan's most serious rival among the designers of the first Chicago School of Architecture was John Wellborn Root. In his Chicago Hotel of 1891, later the Great Northern, at the northeast corner of Dearborn Street and Jackson Boulevard, Root sought to equal the Auditorium with an edifice that would combine under one roof a hotel, an office building, and a theatre. The hotel (below left) was one of Chicago's most sophisticated structures, carrying forward the brilliant economy of materials first evidenced by Root in the Montauk of 1882 and brought to full fruition in the Monadnock designed in 1889. Its steel and wrought-iron frame was sheathed with an undulating brick and terra-cotta surface of powerful unity topped by a Richardsonian cornice. The hotel makes one wonder what the completed plan would have been like, but Root's untimely death at forty-one in 1891 prevented him from finishing the project.

The Great Northern Theatre and Office Building (left) was a pseudo-Gothic structure by Root's partner, Daniel H. Burnham. With its completion in 1895, the Great Northern complex fronted on Quincy Street, as well as on Dearborn and Jackson. Its theatre (right), a throwback to the Moresque style popularized in the 1870s by Sir Charles Eastlake's *Household Taste,* opened on November 9, 1896 with Henry Miller in *Heartsease.* Two years later the theatre, whose plan is shown above, became a vaudeville house. The Great Northern Hotel was demolished in 1940, the office building and theatre in 1961.

14154

J.W. TAYLOR
CHICAGO.

The early years of the twentieth
century saw Chicago second only to
New York in importance as a theatre
town. Among the most famous, or
infamous, theatres built at this time
was the Colonial on Randolph
Street (right). When it opened in
November 1903 it was called the
Iroquois, but just a month later on
December 30, 596 people, many of
them children, died in a fire there. It
was renamed the Colonial in 1905.
Neither the facade nor the lobby
(opposite below) was seriously
damaged by the blaze. In the design
of the lobby the theatre's architect
Benjamin H. Marshall, much
influenced by the new Edwardian
playhouses of London, assembled a
dazzling display of varicolored
marble, bronze lamp standards, and
brightly gilded cartouches, swags,
and Ionic capitals. The Colonial was
demolished in 1924-25 and
replaced by the Oriental movie
house.

In 1923 C. Howard Crane and
Kenneth Franzheim designed two
highly formal, classical theatres, the
Selwyn and the Harris, side by side
on Dearborn Street (right above).
The decor of the auditorium of the
Harris (opposite above) was based
on fifteenth-century Florentine
motifs. Its handsome, walnut
paneling was embellished with
elaborate intarsia in gold, while its
Italian Renaissance ceiling was in
full color. Crane and Franzheim
designed every detail, including the
lighting fixtures and the crimson
velvet stage curtains and draperies
of the boxes. After the Second
World War both the Harris and the
Selwyn became movie theatres.

Dance Halls

Chicago was, from the first, a toddling town. "We had not been here an hour before an invitation to a public ball was courteously sent to us by the managers," Charles Fenno Hoffman, a proper Boston lawyer, wrote in 1834. Hoffman

Above is the cover of a 1932 brochure used to promote the Aragon. Its theme was a familiar one: "Dance and Stay Young."

enjoyed himself, which was no mean test of the powers of Terpischore, for the man had but one leg. Hoffman reported that the ball was held in a room with unfinished walls and a white-washed ceiling.

Later, generations of Chicagoans and visitors could dance in rooms a good deal more finished, such as the Aragon (opposite) which opened in 1926 on West Lawrence Avenue. The ballroom was the brain child of the Karzas brothers, William and Andrew. Designed by Boyd Hill of Huszagh and Hill to resemble the courtyard of a Moorish castle, it appealed to a generation that adored anything vaguely Spanish. Built to hold 8,000 people, its dance floor, resting on a cushion of cork, felt, and springs, vibrated to the music of bands such as those of Freddy Martin and Wayne King. Overhead, hidden projectors created what the dance hall's literature described as "a balmy, languorous night in Old Spain—the heavens strewn with blinking stars and moving clouds."

In recent years the Aragon has been used for rock concerts.

In 1905 Chicago witnessed the opening of one of America's most elaborate amusement parks, the fourteen-acre Beaux-Arts White City at 63rd Street and South Park Avenue (below). The work of the New York builder Edward C. Boyce, its ballroom, seen above in 1915, lasted through the 1940s, long after most of White City had been torn down. Paul Biese who played there was one of Chicago's most popular bandleaders.

Movies

Chicago seems to have always been a city of deeply rooted ethnic neighborhoods. One of them, the Jewish ghetto whose spine was West 12th Street, later renamed Roosevelt Road, played a key role in making Chicago the cradle of the American movie palace. The district was rich in theatres, including Glickman's Palace at Blue Island Avenue, the Midwestern showcase of Yiddish drama in the first two decades of this century. In the years just before the First World War, Roosevelt Road's playhouses fascinated young writers such as Sherwood Anderson and Maxwell Bodenheim, whose own dramas were just beginning to appear on

Chicago's experimental stages such as the Players' Workshop. Two of them, Ben Hecht and Kenneth Sawyer Goodman, who had collaborated on a number of successful plays—among them "The Hero of Santa Maria" and "The Homecoming"—thought that they might establish an important, living theatre there. Hecht recalled that lost dream years later in his memoir *Gaily, Gaily:* "Kenneth and I toured the city in his four-cylinder automobile looking for an ideal site for our Peoples' Theatre. We found one in the Jewish ghetto around Maxwell Street. Kenneth assured me that it would take only a few hundred thousand dollars . . . to

make Chicago one of the world's theatre art centers."

The catalyst in the transformation of legitimate theatres into movie houses was the Balaban family, seen below on the stage of their Circle Theatre at 3241 West Roosevelt Road. Abe, number 4, sang; sister Ida, number 6, played the piano and married Sam Katz who eventually made up the second half of the immortal Balaban and Katz combination; Barney, number 3, was the behind-the-scenes organizer. The Circle opened as a legitimate theatre in 1909, but by 1913 the celluloid Rubicon had been crossed and it was showing moving pictures.

The inauguration of the era of the movie palace may be marked by the opening in 1917 of Balaban and Katz's 2,400-seat Central Park (right) at 3535 West Roosevelt Road. The Central Park began the long, rewarding collaboration between Balaban and Katz and the architect brothers, Cornelius W. and George Rapp, who were eventually to design the Balaban mausoleum. The Central Park's scenery, side stages, and curtain were created by Frank Cambria, a master of stage show design.

Shown above is the marquee of the Central Park in 1940. The theatre has been used as, among other things, a church.

The full flowering of the movie palace came in February 1921 with the completion of the Balaban and Katz 4,000-seat Tivoli at 63rd and Cottage Grove Avenue. The six-story facade (left) gave an intriguing hint of the opulence within by means of its huge window which revealed draperies of purple velvet and gold kid appliqué. The fine interiors, such as that of the mezzanine (below) with its marble Corinthian columns and a ceiling painted after the style of Jean Homore Fragonard, was closely supervised by the architects, Rapp and Rapp. The furniture was supplied by the New York firm of Harold Rambusch. The theatre had a profound influence on South Siders: " 'Say, Dan,' said Vinc Curley. 'Yeah,' said O'Doul, as he stood in a corner, sheiked out, and unrumpled. 'Want to go to the Tivoli tomorrow afternoon?' "— James T. Farrell, *The Young Manhood of Studs Lonigan*. The Tivoli's tomorrows ended in the 1960s.

The pride that Chicago theatre owners took in their decor is evident in the 1930 photograph (above) of the opening of the Century at Clark Street and Diversey Parkway. The cabinet that the two policemen are guarding was said to be worth $22,000. The Century, which began life in 1924 as the Diversey, is now a shopping mall.

Rapp and Rapp's Palace of 1926 on West Randolph Street was lavishly furnished even by 1920s movie house standards. A stunning white and gold composition said to have been modeled on a Neopolitan palazzo, its lobby (right) was lit by Venetian chandeliers and wall sconces, and was furnished with fine French and Italian pieces. The white marble statue was carved especially for the theatre in Italy. The mezzanine (above) boasted a grand piano which was used to entertain patrons waiting for the next show.

When the 4,325 seat Uptown, whose proscenium is shown at right, opened in 1925 at Broadway and Lawrence Avenue it was the largest movie theatre in the United States. The Uptown was advertised as a "palace of . . . Old Spain" and in its sixty-five-foot-high lobby (opposite), Rapp and Rapp created a truly stupendous space. Marshall Field and Company was responsible for the decorating and $62,000 was spent on draperies alone. Sadly, where Garbo once whispered, rock music now resounds.

In the 1920s Chicagoans adored movie stars the way their parents had adored Sarah Bernhardt. Below, Mary Pickford arrives at the University of Chicago's Bartlett Gymnasium for a charity dance in 1916. The Illinois poet Vachel Lindsay paid tribute to "America's Sweetheart" with a poem that began: "Mary Pickford, doll divine . . ." and went on to lament her rumored desertion of the silver screen for the stage:

> Fly, O song, to her today,
> Like a cowboy cross the land.
> Snatch her from Belasco's hand
> And that prison called Broadway.

48

IV MANY MANSIONS

In an early chapter of Theodore Dreiser's novel *The Titan,* set in Chicago in the 1880s and '90s, there is a passage detailing the expectations of the financier Frank Cowperwood and his wife that reveals much about the city they hoped to conquer: "Most of all at present their thoughts centered upon Chicago society, the new house, which by now had been contracted for, and what it would do to facilitate their introduction and standing." Since the late 1830s, when William Butler Ogden imported the city's first architect, John Van Osdel, to build him an impressive residence, the mansions of Chicago have played an important role in proclaiming the financial and thus the social security of Chicagoans. Boston Brahmins might be content to huddle in Beacon Hill's diminutive federal houses and Knickerbocker New Yorkers might relish remaining in the Greek Revival relics around Washington Square, but that was not the tone of a city as brash and as new as Chicago. Its grandees studded the metropolis from Hyde Park to Prairie Avenue to Astor Street and the northern suburbs with palaces built in a rich and astonishing variety of styles. Some critical visitors were repelled by what they perceived to be architectural chaos, but they failed to see the deeper reality, that here was a celebration of individualism, here was freedom from the narrow strictures of an academy, be it royal or Beaux-Arts.

The almost infinite variety of Chicago mansions is revealed in these two photographs. At left is the dining room in the townhouse that David Adler designed in 1921 at 1406 Astor Street for Joseph T. Ryerson, son of Edward Ryerson of the Inland Steel Corporation. The house, a Beaux-Arts monument, was in an elegant, restrained Louis XVI style. With this circular dining room Adler created an impeccable late eighteenth-century neoclassical interior. Every historical detail is handled with skillful certainty, including the mirror frames carved to give the effect of depth and perspective, the simplified paneling, and the cornice with its deep denticulations.

A sharp contrast is offered below by the entrance hall fireplace with its built-in flanking seats that John Wellborn Root of Burnham and Root designed in 1887 at 104 East Bellevue Place. In its serious tone, its straightforward treatment of materials, Root reveals his mastery of the nuances of the arts and crafts movement. One can almost hear William Morris, the high priest of that movement, making one of his thundering pronouncements: "For I tell you that unless you are resolved to have good and rational architecture, it is, once again, useless your thinking about art at all." The house was commissioned by Reginald De Koven, the composer of "Indian Love Song" and "O Promise Me."

Lake Shore Palaces

Potter Palmer has been called the "Father of State Street" but he could, with equal accuracy, be hailed as the "Father of Lake Shore Drive." When in 1882 it was announced that Palmer and his wife, the former Bertha Honoré, intended to build a mansion on the windswept corner of Lake Shore Drive and Banks Street, it is no exaggeration to say, in the words of the well-known song, "they all laughed." No one in his right mind would live in that far north wasteland the wiseacres said. But the laughter had as little effect on the astute Palmer as it did on Thomas Edison or Wilbur and Orville Wright. Palmer had judged that this particular portion of the lake front—the only part not spoiled by railroad tracks—would eventually be enormously attractive as a place of residence and that the district would not be marred by the encroachment of business which was

rapidly driving fashionable Chicagoans away from Michigan Avenue. He was prepared to wait and to take his profit in good time, for Palmer owned no less than 3,000 feet of prime lake-front property in the vicinity of his new house. As was usually the case, Potter Palmer's judgment proved to be sound. By the time he opened his castle in 1885, rich and socially powerful friends, such as William Borden, were planting their own palaces along the Lake Michigan shore.

One of the flagships of Chicago's Lake Michigan palaces was 1000 Lake Shore Drive, seen opposite through the superb gates that the Winslow Company fabricated for the German Building at the Columbian Exposition. Designed by Solon S. Beman, the gray granite, Romanesque forty-one-room castle had been built in the early 1880s for a grain trader, Nathaniel Jones. In 1896 Harold Fowler McCormick, son of the "Reaper King," Cyrus Hall McCormick, and his bride, Edith, daughter of John D. Rockefeller, moved in. Even after their divorce Mrs. McCormick reigned here as one of Chicago's social queens.

A bay of the drawing room (right) shows part of Mrs. McCormick's fine collection of French antiques and oriental art. The Empire Room (below) with its rare objects that had belonged to Napoleon I was Mrs. McCormick's favorite room. The crash of '29 diminished even the Rockefeller-McCormick fortune and in 1932 Mrs. McCormick closed the house and moved across the street to the Drake Hotel. It was opened once more for her funeral in August 1932 and was demolished in 1955.

On the opposite page above is a photograph of Edith Rockefeller-McCormick in the early 1920s when she became known familiarly as Mrs. Rockefeller-McCormick.

Legendary is an overused word but it applies when speaking of the MacVeagh house (right) which stood for less than three decades at 103 Lake Shore Drive. It was one of the last projects of the seminal Boston architect, Henry Hobson Richardson, who had such a profound impact on Louis Sullivan and the other members of the first Chicago School of Architecture. Begun in 1885, the year before Richardson's death, it was completed by the firm of Shepley, Rutan, and Coolidge in 1887.

The mansion was built for the wholesale grocery tycoon, Franklin MacVeagh, and his wife Emily (above). The MacVeaghs were a highly civilized couple and their house reflects their taste. He was Secretary of the Treasury under

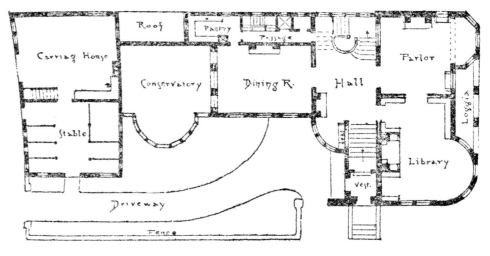

The first floor plan of the MacVeagh house was typical of most lake shore palaces in that the main entrance was not in the facade facing the Drive but opened onto a more protected side street.

President William Howard Taft, founder of the Municipal Art League in Chicago, a supporter of the Art Institute. She was a patron of *Poetry* magazine and active in the American Free Art League.

The entrance to the conservatory (above) and the principal doorway (right) are Richardson in his purest Romanesque vein and recall the perfection of his Trinity Church in Boston and his Sever Hall at Harvard. The house makes an appearance in Margaret Ayer Barners delightful Chicago novel, *Years of Grace:* ''They [the Lesters] lived just around the corner . . . in a grey stone fortress, built by Richardson, the great Eastern architect.'' The fortress fell in 1914.

Though it was officially called the ballroom, this splendid white and gold chamber at the top of the MacVeagh house was more often used for concerts. The frieze of painted fabric running around the walls above the windows was placed there to improve the acoustics. For dances, an orchestra played in the gallery at the far end of the room. Shepley, Rutan, and Coolidge, the Boston firm that designed the room, derived its inspiration from a number of French palaces, particularly Fontainebleau, and the influence is celebrated by the *fleur de lis* surrounding the fireplace. It would be difficult to disagree with the opinion expressed by the architect and critic Russell Sturgis in his 1896 monograph on Shepley, Rutan, and Coolidge that "this is a room of extraordinary beauty."

The Potter Palmers knew the importance of an impressive entrance. If the battlemented exterior of their castle at 1350 Lake Shore Drive had not sufficiently awed their visitor, then the liveried butler who opened the massive door, which had no knob on the outside, most probably did. If even that had not worked, then the great hall, viewed at right, looking towards the second story landing, would undoubtedly do the trick. It most certainly did in Upton Sinclair's bitter novel of Chicago, *The Jungle*, when the hapless Jurgis Rudkus is dragged there by the fictional son of the house: "The place where they stood was dimly lighted; but he could see a vast hall, with pillars fading into the darkness above, and a great staircase opening at the far end of it."

The work of the firm of Silsbee and Kent with furnishings by Herter Brothers of New York, the hall was octagonal in shape, some thirty feet across, with six doorways leading to six important apartments. In the flamboyant manner of the 1880s it unabashedly borrowed design elements from a variety of sources, English Gothic, Moorish, and Romanesque among them. The foliated iron work filling the arches of the arcades followed German patterns, while the important marble mosaic floor in the hall was of Italian workmanship. H. H. Richardson thought that the chamber's vast stained-glass dome, which rose above a bracketed cove, was one of the handsomest bits of architecture in America.

Shortly before the castle and its half block of stables and service buildings was razed in 1950 to make way for an apartment building, there was one last night of glory. A glittering debut party was held in the principal rooms for a great-granddaughter of the Potter Palmers. When it was over an era ended for Chicago just as surely as it had for New York when, in 1940, the last Vanderbilt house on Fifth Avenue closed.

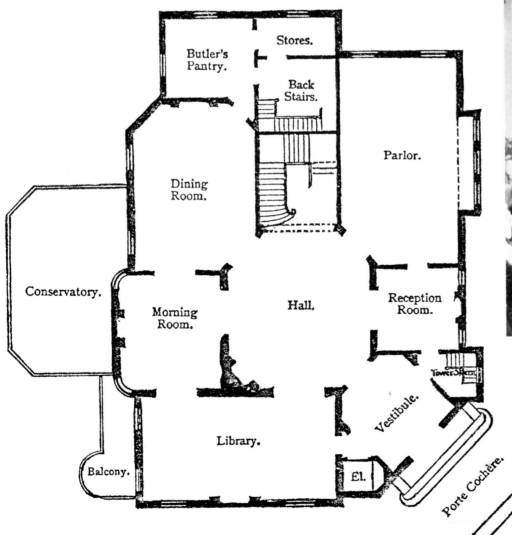

Butler's Pantry.

Stores.

Back Stairs.

Dining Room.

Parlor.

Conservatory.

Morning Room.

Hall.

Reception Room.

Library.

Vestibule.

Balcony.

El.

Porte Cochère.

A brougham replete with coachman and footman waits near the porte-cochère of the Potter Palmer castle (above left). The exterior of the house was designed by Cobb and Frost and was completed in 1883. Built of Connecticut brownstone and Amherst, Ohio, sandstone, the "zebra" effect of the castle was found startling by many people. Standing on this porte-cochère in October 1891, Mrs. Ulysses S. Grant viewed the remainder of the Army of Tennessee with its tattered battle flags as it marched by for the unveiling of the Grant Monument in Lincoln Park. Far left is the house's ground-floor plan.

The library facing Lake Michigan (above) was Potter Palmer's favorite retreat. Of English oak in a Flemish Renaissance design, the room, with its bookcases and other furnishings, was the creation of Herter Brothers. A bright touch of color was added by the long mural painted by Gabriel Ferrier, depicting Romeo and Juliet and Marguerite and Faust.

Left is a rare 1890s photograph of Bertha Honoré Palmer by the distinguished photographer F. Holland Day.

The Palmer dining room (above), also by Herter Brothers, featured San Domingan mahogany woodwork, an Elizabethan sideboard, and a frieze of cupids cavorting in Arcadia by the American artist John Elliott. The twenty-two- by forty-two-foot drawing room (right) is in the Louis XV style it was given by the Herters. The desired effect of grandeur was achieved by placing gilt furniture on a mosaic pavement of sprays of pink roses and under an elaborate ceiling with a mural of playful cherubs painted by Perraud.

The drawing room is seen at left after it was redesigned in the 1920s in a far more chaste English Chippendale style by David Adler for Mr. and Mrs. Potter Palmer II. Shown above is one end of Mrs. Palmer's seventy-five-foot-long picture gallery. The room, which was added after the house was completed, had velvet-covered walls with wainscoting and columns of dark red Numidian marble. On the far wall are some of Mrs. Palmer's Claude Monets, including the famous haystack series of 1891.

61

Houses of Talent

"But in the town of Chicago which one had been told was populated exclusively by vulgar people, I discovered more amiable men, men more considerate and more truly civil, than in New York," announced the French travel writer, Jules Huret, in his *L'Amérique Modern* of 1911. As a city, Chicago had more than its share of houses built by superior architects for clients who were both civil and perceptive. These residences were not on the scale of the Lake Shore palaces, but they were, in a double sense, because of their design and their inhabitants, houses of talent.

In his novel, *Prairie Avenue,* Arthur Meeker's leading character Ned Ramsay observes: "Then, suddenly the houses grew bigger and grander, the elm trees taller, the gardens more spacious, and they were in Prairie Avenue." The presence of the emporium emperor, Marshall Field (left), on the avenue undoubtedly had a good deal to do with its grandeur, though it also gathered some stardust from the presence of the Pullmans of Pullman, the Armours of Armour, and the Kimballs of the Kimball piano.

When in 1876 Field commissioned the New York architect Richard Morris Hunt to design him a house, Hunt was the most renowned architect in America. Educated in Paris at the prestigious Ecole des Beaux-Arts under the famed Hector Lefuel, Hunt took America by storm. What is particularly interesting about the red brick and sandstone house that he built for Field at 1906 Prairie Avenue was that it was in a quite pure French Second Empire style as though Hunt were dreaming of his Paris years two decades earlier. Later in his career Hunt would design opulent palazzi for clients such as John Jacob Astor and Cornelius Vanderbilt, but for Marshall Field he was all the "conservatism and judiciousness" for which he was originally noted. The house must have suited Field, who was himself all "conservatism and judiciousness," for he lived there until his death in 1906.

The interior of the Field mansion was luxurious but not notably so for a man who was to leave an estate of more than $100,000,000 and whose second wife Delia Caton (far left) could pose happily in a society *tableau vivant* as the Queen of the Peacock Throne. The hall (opposite) had mahogany wainscoting and embossed leather-covered walls that rose to a ceiling frescoed in simple patterns. Field did set a fashion of sorts by using a large number of Renaissance antiques selected by Herter Brothers throughout his house. Before this time most of the "antiques" in Chicago residences were reproductions.

The library (below) had a fine wood-paneled ceiling with decorated cassets and walls hung with dark tapestries. The room's *piece de resistance* was the fireplace at the far end with pillars of polished marble framing an overmantle which held a stained glass window depicting one of the muses. Marshall Field's favorite painting, Jean Louis Meissonier's "The Outpost," hung in this room.

In 1937 the New Bauhaus, made up of refugees from the original German Bauhaus, was reestablished in this Beaux-Arts structure; in 1955 Marshall Field's mansion was razed.

The library (above) was, appropriately, the heart of Edward E. Ayer's house at 2 East Banks Street. A lumberman who owned vast tracts of land in Mexico and Arizona, Ayer made a fortune in railroad materials. His real passion, though, was books, especially those dealing with the exploration and colonization of the Western Hemisphere. In 1911 he presented some 14,000 rare volumes on these and related subjects, together with a generous endowment for new purchases to the Newberry Library of which he was a trustee. In witty recognition of Ayer's Mexican holdings, the architect of his house, John Wellborn Root of Burnham and Root, decorated the library fireplace with Mexican onyx.

In the entrance hall (opposite) Root, who is shown at right as he looked at the beginning of his architectural practice in the early 1870s, expressed in concrete form what he later expressed in words in *Scribner's* magazine. The article was entitled "The City House in the West" and the relevant passage is:

"In the growth of the house-plan from the earlier types the first great change began with the hall. This, originally a narrow passage, of no service for living and with few possibilities for decorative treatment, has been expanded, and made of practical value in several ways, becoming not only a large and picturesque room of itself, but serving admirably as a general reception-room or rendezvous for family and guests . . . "

In this hall of 1885, Root drew his inspiration from the "living-halls" designed by Richardson for dwellings such as the Paine house in Waltham, Massachusetts, and from the British architects like Norman Shaw who were deeply influenced by the arts and crafts movement. The room, with its fine wooden ceiling, its bold metal work, and its staircase flowing gracefully around the beautifully designed restrained fireplace, was one of Chicago's, if not America's, supreme domestic interiors. Lamentably, in 1965 the Ayer house fell before the wrecker's ball.

Nineteenth- and early twentieth-century Chicago was a city of Medicean collectors but none more so than Martin A. Ryerson, son of Martin Ryerson, a lumber baron who was himself an enthusiastic supporter of the Art Institute. Ryerson's gray stone Romanesque dwelling at 4851 Drexel Boulevard (below right) stood on one of the South Side's most impressive residential streets. It is very like the house that awed Bigger Thomas in Richard Wright's *Native Son* when he went there for a job: "He came to Drexel Boulevard and began to look for 4605. When he came to it, he stopped and stood before a high, black, iron picket fence . . ."

Designed by the firm of Treat and Foltz in 1886, it was truly a treasure house. The library (right) with its superb Renaissance paintings, sculpture, and furnishings was filled with things that the Ryersons had bought on their travels throughout Europe. The room, indeed the entire mansion, belongs to the era when J. P. Morgan was assembling his great library in New York; when Isabella Stewart Gardner was composing her Venetian palace in Boston; and when Henry E. Huntington was putting together his staggering collection of books and art outside Los Angeles.

Ryerson's sure and wide-ranging taste may be judged from the fact that in 1890, through the purchase of the Demidoff and May collections, he made possible the first exhibition of old masters in Chicago. Twenty-two years later on one day, November 11, 1912, he facilitated the purchase by the Art Institute of no less than eight masterpieces that he had personally selected, including a Goya, a Renoir, a Degas, and two Monets.

Unfortunately, almost alone among major American cities, Chicago has not preserved a single residence where it is possible to see how its great private collections looked when their owners were alive. The Ryerson house has most recently served as a Franciscan monastery.

66

Shown above is Mrs. Ryerson's bedroom on the second floor with a Monet ''Water Lilies'' of 1906 on the wall next to the fireplace. At left is the painting which is now in the Art Institute.

At right is Mr. and Mrs. Ryerson with Claude Monet, on the left, in his famous garden at Giverny outside Paris where the ''Water Lilies'' was painted. The photograph was taken shortly before the First World War.

Among Chicago's numerous lumber kings, one of the most prominent was William Owen Goodman, seen above in front of his house at 5026 South Greenwood Avenue in the then elite South Side suburb of Kenwood. An 1880s Queen Anne composition by Treat and Foltz, its entrance hall (right) was decorated in the fashionable Renaissance style. The house's heavy, elaborately carved furniture, such as the sofa (right below), was supplied by the Brooks Household Art Company of Cleveland, Ohio, and was inspired by German and Flemish models. The Goodmans' son, Kenneth Sawyer Goodman, a promising playwright, died of pneumonia in 1918 while serving in the Navy. His parents gave the Goodman Theatre to the Art Institute as a memorial.

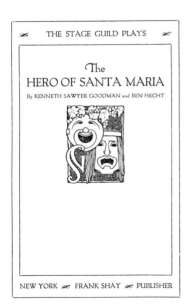

Cover of the script of a play first produced in 1917 that Kenneth Sawyer Goodman wrote with Ben Hecht.

At right above is the Queen Anne dining room (in the Goodman residence) with its impressive Jacobean ceiling and fireplace. The pastoral painting was considered appropriate art in a room where one dined.

The bedroom (below right), most likely the young Kenneth Sawyer Goodman's, is an interesting example of the irregularly shaped rooms so popular at this time. The William Morris-style chair in the foreground reveals the profound influence that the arts and crafts movement had in Chicago by the turn-of-the-century.

In 1914 Howard Van Doren Shaw completed for the Goodmans an impressive federal-style residence (right) on Astor Street, the North Side's most fashionable residential thoroughfare. Though the design of the new house was very different from the old one, the drawing room (above) was furnished largely with pieces brought from Greenwood Avenue, a triumph of sentiment over fashion. The Goodman house has been cut up into apartments.

V PRAIRIE PAVILIONS AND CASTLES IN THE AIR

It is ironic that the first collection of verse published in Chicago, a miscellany by the now forgotten William Asbury Kenyon, should have celebrated, among other things, the joy of escaping the urban hurly-burly:

> No hermit's cave, no crowded hive,
>   No storm-tossed prison lone;
> But life at ease, in joy's own breeze,
>   A prairie cot my own.

Ever since Kenyon published his poem in 1845, Chicagoans have been diligently seeking their own prairie cots. As fast as the developing railways, street car lines, and highways permitted, they have been pushing out onto the prairie to their pavilions in Riverside, Oak Park, and Lake Forest.

Coinciding with this rush outwards has been one upwards, limited only by the speed with which the iron-and-steel-framed skyscraper could break new altitude barriers. Though these high-rise apartments might have their physical foundations in the city, their psychological base was elsewhere. Cole Porter knew of what he sang when he described a 90th floor apartment as a "regal eagle's nest." The ideal of the glittering peaks of North Michigan Avenue and Lake Shore Drive was not a townhouse, but a castle in the air.

Villas

With this house for John Farson on Home Avenue in Oak Park (below), George W. Maher employed the spacious sweep of its broad front porch to emphasize and celebrate the space provided by a large suburban building lot. Maher's delight in horizontality marks him as a member of the Prairie School, and he had, in fact, been a colleague of its leading practitioner, Frank Lloyd Wright, in the office of Joseph L. Silsbee. The Wicker furniture displayed in such profusion on the porch was very much in vogue when the house was completed in 1897.

In the ancient Roman world an annual summer's rustication in the country was considered an essential feature of the civilized life. Appropriately, the finest expression in the Chicago suburbs of a country villa was built on the Roman model. It even had a Roman name, Villa Turicum. That the house was designed in this style is symbolic of an important watershed in taste in Chicago. Shortly after the turn-of-the-century when Harold McCormick and his wife, the former Edith Rockefeller, decided to build in the exclusive north shore suburb of Lake Forest they went to none other than Frank Lloyd Wright, who projected for them a grandiose but contemporary-style dwelling. Already, though, Chicago's rich were turning away from local designers, who, curiously, seemed to them slightly old-fashioned, and were employing East Coast architects who were creating sensational palaces at Newport and on Long Island in a dazzling variety of historical-revival styles. The McCormicks, to the lasting astonishment of Wright, rejected his plans and commissioned the New York Beaux-Arts architect, Charles Adams Platt, to build their house.

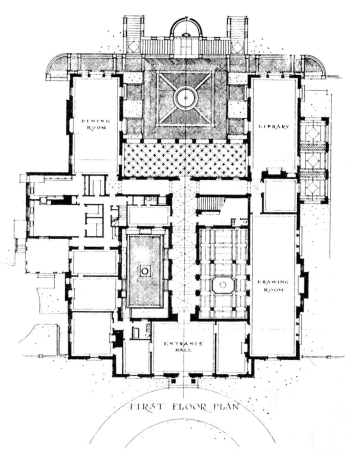

FIRST FLOOR PLAN

What they got was something far different from what Wright had proposed, but there can be no doubt that the forty-four-room villa Platt built between 1907 and 1912 was one of America's most sensational country places. Platt, whose *Italian Gardens* of 1894 was a landmark in the field of landscape design, set his villa (above right) in the midst of 250 lakefront acres of beautifully planned grounds. (The garden front of the villa may be seen at left during one of Mrs. McCormick's 1920s parties.) A man who loved to work in the Italian Renaissance mode, Platt created a drawing room (above) that was a masterpiece of that period with elegant, cool, green marble walls rising to a many-colored coffered ceiling highlighted with gold. The Pompeiian room (right) was a version of the recently excavated Casa Dei Vetti, and its dark-red frescoed walls and antique columns and statues show the sure touch of an architect who was president of the American Academy in Rome.

Villa Turicum, which had cost $5,000,000 to build, was sold in 1947 for $46,000 and was demolished in 1956.

Thomas agency who revolutionized American advertising. The mansion's plan is shown below. Its grounds also included an eighteen-hole golf course which was considered one of the finest in the United States. At right is the Lasker living room, on which Adler collaborated with his sister, the decorator Francis Elkins. Adler's gift for creating impressive architectural spaces is clearly revealed in the hall of the Lasker House (below right) with its faded red tile flooring and its powerful sequence of arches.

After 1926, David Adler turned to other less grand styles, particularly Georgian, for his houses. He and the other architects who built in the vicinity of Lake Forest have left there an exceptional record of wonderful houses cast in an incredible variety of modes. Mark Smith's observation in his 1973 novel, *The Death of the Detective,* sums up the sense of the place very well: "The wealthy lakeshore village of Lake Forest. Wooded, landscaped lakefront estates with lakefront mansions: Mediterranean villas, French chateaus, Scottish castles, English manor houses, Swiss chalets."

Chicago's own genius of the country house was undoubtedly the Ecole des Beaux-Arts educated David Adler, who was a lifelong admirer of the work of Charles Adams Platt. Adler's 1922 house for Mrs. Morse C. Ely in Lake Forest (top) was a striking adaptation of the Pavillion de La Lanterne in Versailles, designed in the seventeenth century by Louis Le Vau. Adler's formal Louis XV entrance hall for the Ely house (above) would most certainly have received the approbation of two of the Beaux-Arts' most effective

spokesmen, Edith Wharton and Ogden Codman, who in *The Decoration of Houses* of 1897 insisted that such spaces be kept simple and advised that their "ornamentation may consist of statues, vases, or busts on pedestals." Originally surrounded by fine trees, the Ely house is now hedged in by a modern subdivision.

Among the last formal French houses David Adler designed was the one he built in 1926, also in Lake Forest, for Albert D. Lasker, the innovative head of the Lord and

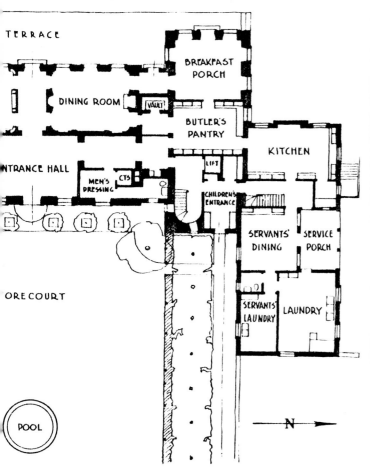

Apartments

A major difficulty faced by the owners of early apartment houses was that their buildings were looked upon as being not quite proper. Young Jane Ward, the heroine of Margaret Ayer Barnes' *Years of Grace*, understands this very well: "Funny French André . . . of whom her mother didn't at all approve, because he was French and a Roman Catholic and went to church in the Holy Name Cathedral and lived in a little flat in the Saint James Apartments . . . " Inexorably, though, the increasing shortage of servants and the skyrocketing value of land in the best residential quarters made apartments first necessary and then fashionable.

An early example of the upper middle class apartment building was the Mentone on the southwest corner of Erie and Dearborn streets (right). The decor of the apartment. in the Mentone of Arthur Dana Wheeler, shown above in his library in 1891, exemplified what Lewis Mumford has called "The Brown

Decades." Yet mixed in with the dark walnut woodwork and rather somber, flocked wallpaper are artistic accessories such as the Japanese screen in the parlor foreground, which demonstrate that Arthur Wheeler had been influenced by aesthetes such as the painter James McNeil Whistler. The Mentone is now a hotel for transients.

Though Solon S. Beman's Pullman Building (right) was built in 1883 at the southwest corner of Michigan Avenue and Adams Street primarily to house the head offices of the Pullman Palace Car Company, its top three floors contained apartments. These flats were much sought after when this nine-story-plus-attic structure was the tallest building in Chicago. Among those who lived in the flats for a time was the utilities promoter Samuel Insull. The apartments, which were connected to the main reception room by the world's first speaking tubes, were converted into offices in 1916. Below is the Pullman Building's covered entrance court on Adams Street. In 1956 this monument of the Romanesque revival was demolished.

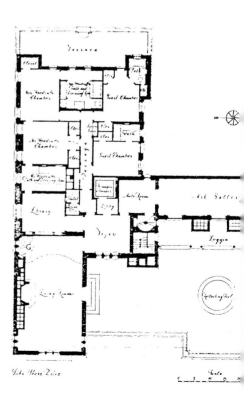

The Woodruff's dining room, in fourteenth-century Gothic style, was decorated with encaustic frescoes of medieval hunting, feasting, commerce, and the Crusades.

After the First World War the construction of luxurious high-rise residential buildings along Lake Shore Drive gave the final stamp of approval to the apartment. Mr. and Mrs. George Woodruff's penthouse, on the 24th and 25th floors of 1500 Lake Shore Drive, was completed in 1930 by the firm of McNally and Quinn and was among Chicago's most sumptuous. Its terrace (above) resembled an Italian villa and even had a bell tower with chimes.

Mrs. Woodruff's Florentine bathroom had light green and gold tiles and pilasters of marble. All the fittings were of solid bronze.

The living room of the Woodruff apartment (left) had a fine Italian Renaissance ceiling that was gilded and painted in soft blue and red tones; a frieze repeated the colors. The windows had shutters of tooled leather also painted in blue and red. A. C. Rindskopf was responsible for decorating the apartment and it was he who designed the furniture and lighting fixtures.

George Woodruff, a banker and La Salle Street promoter, is said to have spent a half million dollars on this penthouse in order to create a suitable setting for his wife, the artist Louise Lentz Woodruff. (Mrs. Woodruff's best known work was *Science Advancing Mankind,* which became the symbol of the 1933 Century of Progress Exposition.) With the Great Depression his bank, the National Bank of the Republic, failed and Woodruff was soon forced to sell his villa in the clouds for a fraction of its cost.

A baronial splendor, much favored in the 1920s, was achieved by decorator Irene Sidley in the dining room (above) of the William Wrigley, Jr. apartment at 1500 Lake Shore Drive, completed in 1929. At a time when many paneled rooms were being imported into the United States, this one stood out as a particularly fine example of English oak linen-fold. It was found in London by the apartment's architect, Edwin H. Clark. The sense of magnificence, appropriate to the family that had made Juicy Fruit and Spearmint household words, was enhanced by the pair of Queen Anne lacquer cabinets and by the superb Oriental carpet. The duplex had twenty-one other rooms.

The introduction of modern taste into apartment decor was often through the bathroom. The one that architect Walter Frazier designed for himself in 1931 (left) in his otherwise traditional Lake Shore Drive flat, sleekly combined chromium with walls of glass painted on the back to achieve a fluted effect.

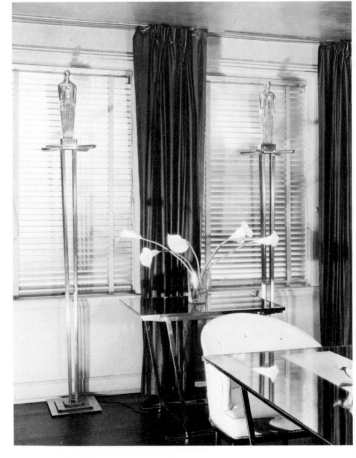

By the end of the 1920s, modern design could be found in an increasing number of apartments in Chicago. In 1929 Thomas Fisher and his wife, the ballerina Ruth Page, achieved a new look for penthouses in their one-room studio (left) atop Holabird and Root's Diana Court at 540 North Michigan Avenue. Its yellow, brick red, and blue decor was the work of the Russian Nicholas Remissoff, who also painted the lissome lion and designed the rugs.

Few Chicago architects had a more sure feeling for the new International Style than Andrew Rebori whose Frank Fisher Apartments at 1209 North State Parkway of 1936 are shown at right. Rebori's entrance court (below right) reveals the two-story glass brick bays that lit the duplexes.

Architect John Wellborn Root, Jr., furnished his late 1920s apartment (left) at 70 East Walton Place, then called the Elizabeth Arden Building, with pieces influenced by French designers such as Maurice Dufrène and Jacques Adnet who worked in a chic, modern, hard-edged style. Root, the son of the John Wellborn Root who was Daniel Burnham's partner, was the senior partner of Holabird and Root. His unfailing good taste found its highest expression in the brittle Art Deco structures his firm designed in the 1920s, such as the Chicago Board of Trade Building on La Salle Street; the Palmolive Building, now the Playboy Club, on North Michigan Avenue; and the obliterated Diana Court.

VI TWO STREETS

The maturity of a city may be seen in the specialization of its streets. The Main Street of a small town embraces the hardware store, the movie, the bank, and the funeral parlor. The true city has streets which become noted for supplying particular types of goods or for their concentration of certain professions and trades or for catering to people's need for entertainment. The mere mention of New York's Broadway conjures up images of theatres, while London's Fleet Street has become a synonym for journalism. Chicago too, as it grew, developed streets that became closely identified with particular facets of existence. Two of them, State and La Salle, were essential to its urban life.

State: Emporiums of Delight

"State Street, the Rue de la Paix of Chicago," trumpeted *The Land Owner,* a Windy City real estate journal in September of 1873. If State Street was that, plus London's Bond Street and New York's Fifth Avenue, the laurels belonged to Potter Palmer who in 1867 had bought almost a mile of the shanty-lined thoroughfare; persuaded Field, Leiter and Company to move there; and

completed the transformation by opening in 1870 a luxurious hotel bearing his name.

Of State Street's many splendid emporiums, few have had a more illustrious history than the jewelers, C. D. Peacock, founded by Elijah Peacock in 1837. At left is an 1883 engraving of the High Victorian interior of Peacock's, then located at State and Washington streets.

Opening day in 1927 (below left) of the new Peacock's in the Palmer House at State and Monroe streets. The interior, by Holabird and Roche, was sheathed in dark green marble from Thessaly in Greece because the color was considered the best background for diamonds. At right is a walnut silver display case of Italian design. The store's exterior with its superb cast bronze Peacock-shaped gates (below) was featured on the firm's 1929 Christmas card.

The keystone of the State Street department stores was Marshall Field's in the center right of this 1890s photograph of State looking north from Washington Street. Field's has had a long history of building and rebuilding. Its first State Street store—the firm was then Field, Leiter and Co.—a white marble palace rented from Potter Palmer, was lost in the Great Fire of 1871. The structure built to replace that was also destroyed by fire scarcely six years later. The very Parisian Second Empire edifice in this photograph was constructed in stages between 1878 and 1892 and was later replaced by the present Marshall Field store in the first decade of this century.

Field's motto "Give the lady what she wants" covered such things as veilings (below left), linen handkerchiefs, and a kid glove cleaning department (below) as seen in these 1904 photographs. The gloves cleaned were most likely the fine French-made Alexandre brand of which Field's was the sole distributor. The high quality of goods that it imported from Europe and the Orient made Field's the nation's leading department store with a wholesale and retail business in excess of $34 million in 1891. The firm's wholesale business was carried on in the historic Romanesque store that Henry Hobson Richardson built for Field in 1885, which filled the entire nearby block bounded by Adams, Quincy, Wells, and Franklin streets.

In its golden years, which stretched from the 1870s to about 1960, when it came to shopping, State Street was indeed the Main Street of the Midwest. Marion Louise Wineman captured those days in one of the verses in her *Chicago Songs* of 1925:

The bell in the clock of the Boston Store
Tolls sweet on the evening air,
For homewending stenos and clerks galore,
And a few hundred thousand, or maybe more
Weary shoppers from Field's and The Fair.

The architectural titan of the State Street stores was the structure that Louis Sullivan began in 1900 for Schlesinger and Mayer, later Carson, Pirie, Scott, and Company. With his Art Nouveau screen (above) which shielded one of the store's third-floor retiring and writing rooms, Sullivan embodied a sentiment expressed in his *Kindergarten Chats:* "Ornament, when creative, spontaneous, is a perfume." The screen, which was removed during a remodeling, consisted of five layers of mahogany sawn in three different patterns. At left is the Carson bus which carried suburbanites from various train stations to the store in 1922.

A window of the now-closed Boston Store displaying 1920s evening gowns (above) employed the fashionable Spanish architecture of the day as background.

Until Wacker Drive forced its closing in 1925, State Street shoppers had the delights of the South Water Street Market at their fingertips. The market, which was essentially a wholesale outlet serving restaurants and shops, was noted for its eggs, butter, fruit, fish, and, above all, for its game which regularly included such exoticisms as leg of mountain sheep, venison and buffalo tongue, and antelope steak. In 1891, for the convenience of retail customers, Burnham and Root were asked to design the Central Market (right). Situated on a wedge-shaped plot at the northeast corner of South Water and State streets, its airy interior was reminiscent of the iron and glass "umbrellas" Victor Baltard designed in 1867 for Paris' own central market, Les Halles.

One of State Street's legends was Kranz's Candy Store (above and right) at 126-132 North State. Its lyrical Art Nouveau interior with bisque marble pillars and Mexican onyx tables was decorated by R. W. Bates of Boston and Abner Crossman of Chicago. Among those who regularly indulged in Kranz's famed sodas and sent as gifts its sugar teddy bears and chocolate mice were Kate Buckingham and Mrs. John T. Pirie. Kranz's went out of business in 1947.

State Street also had office buildings which were particularly favored by doctors and dentists who could take their patients between trips to Kranz's. Among the most baroque structures in the city was the fifteen-story Columbus Memorial, built between 1892–93 by William W. Boyington at the southeast corner of State and Washington streets. Boyington set a high standard of excellence with details such as the bronze elevator grills (opposite).

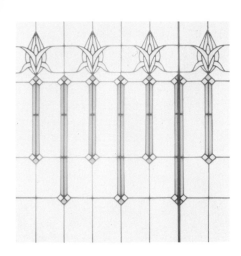

The Republic Building at State and Adams streets revealed Holabird and Roche holding fast to the ideals of the first Chicago School of Architecture with an almost undecorated, gleaming white tower. Originally thirteen-stories-high when completed in 1905, six more were added to it in 1909. The Republic's white marble lobby (right) and its pale blue and white art glass windows (above) were objects of grace. The Columbus Memorial Building was destroyed in 1959, the Republic in 1961.

La Salle: Halls of Commerce

When the Board of Trade opened its rooms in the new Chamber of Commerce building on La Salle Street in 1865, a *Chicago Tribune* reporter with a little classical learning recalled the Roman goddess of vegetation and dubbed them collectively the "Altar of Ceres." The designation was an apt one, for although the grandiose banks and office blocks which then and later lined La Salle Street might appear to be constructed of granite, marble, and bronze, to the cognizant they were made of the wheat, corn, and oats bought and sold on the floor of the Board of Trade. It is no accident that the Board's modern skyscraper home is still crowned by a statue of the ancient goddess.

Shown below is the Chamber of Commerce building at the southeast corner of Washington and La Salle streets as it burned during the Great Chicago Fire of October 1871. The tall windows of the second floor indicate the Board of Trade rooms. Designed by Edward Burling of Lemont limestone in a manner termed "decidedly composite," it was considered the most substantial structure in the city.

Three days after the fire the directors of the Board of Trade made plans to rebuild on the same site. Their spacious Italianate chamber shown at right in this extremely rare stereopticon view, was designed by John Cochrane and Charles Miller. Cochrane was a noted hospital architect, and his credits include Cook County Hospital, old Michael Reese, and the Rush Medical College. The structure was dedicated by Mayor Joseph Medill on October 9, 1872, the first anniversary of the conflagration.

This room, by means of the telegraph and the Atlantic cable, controlled the price of grain throughout the world for more than a decade.

The importance of the business of La Salle Street to Chicagoans is summed up quite well in Janet Ayer Fairbanks' fluffy 1910 drawing room comedy, *In Town and Other Conversations:* "Mrs. Vane (a society matron: 'What with so many hotels opening now, pretty restaurants, and the opera here for so long, I feel as if I were in another city.' Webber (a writer): 'It isn't in the least like Chicago; we are forgetting all about La Salle Street.' Alexander (a stock broker): 'As long as La Salle Street pays the bills, you can afford to forget it.' "

A view down La Salle Street in 1906 (above) with Burnham and Root's rugged Rookery on the left and William W. Boyington's Board of Trade building of 1885 at the end of the street.

Boyington's vast trading room (right above) measured 174 by 155 feet and was more than five stories high. Decorated with frescoes by Italian artists depicting various aspects of history and commerce, it was deemed to be in the Renaissance style. The pits in the foreground where board members stood to trade in different types of grain gave Frank Norris the title for his great Chicago novel, *The Pit*.

The room was often a seething center of activity as it was in September 1888 when Benjamin P. Hutchinson, "Old Hutch," cornered wheat. That exploit was celebrated in a none-too-flattering verse:

In dealing in "Change" whether
    little or much,
All wholesomely fear the insatiate
    Hutch;
O'er eyes of the sharpest he
    "pulleth the wool,"
'Mid "bulls" as a "bear," and 'mid
    "bears" as a "bull,"
How plaintive the tone as crieth
    each mourner,
He'll find—thank the Lord—in
    heaven no corner.

A telling contrast to Boyington's romantic room is presented by Holabird and Root's glittering glass and black and white marble Art Deco lobby in the present Board of Trade building (right), which replaced Boyington's edifice in 1929.

The world-famed second-floor trading room (below) of Adler and Sullivan's Chicago Stock Exchange Building displayed some of Louis Sullivan's most splendid designs. When the room was inaugurated on May 1, 1894, it was considered the finest such facility in the country. To provide an unobstructed view in the 64- by 81-foot chamber, Dankmar Adler designed yet another of his innovative steel frames which carried with ease the eleven floors above it.

Light was supplied both by the ceiling of art glass skylights from the Wenz Art Glass Company, and by carbon filiament lamps, some of which were set around the *faux marbre* columns with their brightly gilt capitals. The glory of the room was its stencil decoration, which employed some sixty-five shades of color with green and ochre predominating.

The celebrated building at the southwest corner of La Salle and Washington streets which held the room was inexcusably demolished in 1972. The chamber itself, as shown here, has been sensitively restored by the architectural firm of Vinci-Kenny, and now stands in The Art Institute of Chicago.

"Here, of all her cities, throbbed the true life—the true power and spirit of America . . . arrogant in the new-found knowledge of its giant strength, prodigal of its wealth, infinite in its desires." Nowhere is Frank Norris' description of Chicago in *The Pit* better illustrated than in the astonishing banks of La Salle Street. The skylighted main room of the Continental and Commercial National Bank at 208 South La Salle (above) was begun in 1914 by D. H. Burnham and Company and completed by the successor firm of Graham, Burnham and Company.

Even more awesome is the chief banking room of the Continental Illinois Bank of 1924 at 231 South La Salle (left and above). The firm of Graham, Anderson, Probst, and White, the architects of the Wrigley Building and Union Station, gave the room a fillip of decorative richness by placing a splendid, gold-splashed coffered ceiling above its gigantic marble Ionic columns. The murals over the grand staircase (left) are by Jules Guérin and celebrate the commerce of the world. This room, still intact, is undoubtedly one of the temples of the American classical tradition.

VII
CLUBLAND

"A club in a metropolis is a positive necessity to the social and business man," wrote Ward McAllister, the inventor of New York's "400," in his preface to William Van Rensselaer Miller's book of 1896, *Select Organizations in the United States*. As life in Chicago became more settled and regularized, this "necessity" led to the founding of the Chicago Club and the Standard in the 1860s. In the next decade they were joined by the Calumet, the Union League, and the Iroquois. The models were inevitably the old established clubs of the east, such as Boston's Somerset and New York's Union, and their precursors across the sea in London. If men felt the need for clubs, so did women, and, alongside their male counterparts, were born the Fortnightly and the Chicago Woman's Club.

The most aristocratic Chicago club of its day was the Calumet, organized in 1878 with the avowed purpose of preserving the city's early history. The club's name is derived from the French word for the American Indian peace pipe (above). On its roster of distinguished members was Mayor John Wentworth; Chicago's first architect, John Van Osdel; and meat packer Philip D. Armour.

The Calumet's clubhouse (opposite) at the northeast corner of Michigan Avenue and Twentieth Street, was designed by Burnham and Root, both of whom were club members, and was completed in 1883. It was substantially rebuilt after a fire in 1892 by Charles Sumner Frost of the firm of Cobb and Frost. The Calumet's rooms,

such as the one shown at right, had a decidedly masculine air right down to the strategically placed brass spittoons. This room was one of many used for cards and other such games, a form of amusement to which club members were so addicted that a rule was passed strictly forbidding "games" after midnight Saturday and all day Sunday.

The Calumet Club had a notable early collection of paintings presented by A. A. Munger, and its annual art show was one of the first regularly held in Chicago. The other notable annual event at the club was its Old Settlers Reception for those who had resided in Chicago prior to 1840. The Calumet Club was disbanded in 1915 and its clubhouse has been demolished.

Onwentsia Hunt Ball

The Onwentsia in Lake Forest, one of Chicago's leading golf clubs, like the Calumet took for its name a word with Indian connotations. "Onwentsia" means a meeting place of braves and squaws. From 1895 it occupied the former home of architect Henry Ives Cobb, the head of Cobb and Frost, where this hunt ball dinner was photographed in 1905.

The Onwentsia, with its membership of Farwells, Deerings, Keeps, McCormicks, Smiths, and Swifts, has been a pioneer in the Midwest, not only of golf but of tennis and polo as well. The old clubhouse was replaced in 1928.

Since it was organized in 1869 the Standard Club has been Chicago's leading Jewish social club. Over the years its members have included some of the nation's most prominent businessmen such as Union Stockyards founder Nelson Morris and advertising pioneer Albert D. Lasker, the Florsheims of shoes, the Spiegels of mail order catalogues, and the Blocks of Inland Steel. Though the club has been a center of Jewish philanthropy, its generosity has known no religious barriers. At the

University of Chicago alone, buildings given by Standard Club members include Mandel Hall, Rosenwald Hall, Epstein Clinic, Goldblatt Cancer Research Center, the Regenstein Library, and the Pritzker School of Medicine.

The Standard's flag-festooned first clubhouse on the southwest corner of Michigan Avenue and Thirteenth Street (left below), which it occupied from 1870 to 1889, is seen in this 1893 photograph taken after it had become the headquarters of the Grand Army of the Republic. Left above is an interior view of the club following the great Chicago Fire when it was taken over by the city's Relief and Aid Society. The Standard is now located on South Plymouth Court.

"The races in question were soon to open at Washington Park, on the South Side, and were considered quite society affairs . . ." The social importance of Washington Park, implied in this quotation from Theodore Dreiser's *Sister Carrie* was not an exaggeration. Though the track's grandstand was open to all for the price of a dollar, its clubhouse was for members only, among whom were Samuel W. Allerton, N. K. Fairbank, and Gen. Philip Sheridan, who was a club president. Below, a fashionably dressed throng watches the American Derby early in this century from the clubhouse enclosure. The grand old course, whose buildings were designed by Solon S. Beman, conducted meetings at Sixty-first Street and South Park Avenue from the mid-1880s until 1908.

Love. Founded in a room at the Chicago Club in 1883, the Fortnightly's elegant Georgian premises on Bellevue Place just off Lake Shore Drive (right) were built in 1892 by the famed New York architects, McKim, Mead, and White for Bryan Lathrop, a real estate wizard who was a founder of the Chicago Orchestra Association.

The guiding hand behind the club's decoration was Mrs. John Alden Carpenter, who was known as Chicago's Elsie de Wolfe, and whose credits included Elizabeth Arden's New York salon. The club's exterior (below right), a vigorous

"In the previous decade it had founded its first two clubs, the Chicago and the Standard, the first a gentile organization, on March 25, 1869 . . . " wrote Lloyd Lewis in *Chicago: The History of Its Reputation.* After occupying quarters in various antique mansions, the Chicago Club moved into a Venetian Gothic structure at 12 East Monroe Street (above), opposite the Palmer House, that Treat and Foltz designed for it. The interior was an Eastlake mélange of various historical styles popularized by the Centennial Exposition held in Philadelphia in 1876, the year the clubhouse was completed. The rooms were to become familiar to a generation of Chicagoans as De Jonghe's Restaurant, which later bought the edifice from the club.

By the 1890s the Chicago, now indisputably the *ne plus ultra* of the city's social clubs, had outgrown its home and in 1893 it moved into

Burnham and Root's wonderful old Romanesque Art Institute (right) at Michigan Avenue and Van Buren Street. At its round "millionaires" table could be found almost daily Marshall Field, George M. Pullman, Levi Z. Leiter, and Robert Todd Lincoln. The building collapsed during remodelling in 1929 and the members built a new clubhouse on the site.

"There are, perhaps I should explain, at least ten thousand women's clubs in Chicago . . . But the only ones that count socially are the Fortnightly, the Friday, and the Scribblers," proclaimed Arthur Meeker in 1955 in *Chicago with*

interpretation of English Georgian architecture, was originally enhanced by graceful iron balconies.

Though it was most certainly social with a membership that included Mrs. Potter Palmer, Mrs. John J. Glessner, and Mrs. Charles Henrotin, the Fortnightly also tried to maintain an intellectual tone and was deeply involved in the women's suffrage movement. Among its more eccentric members was Edith Rockefeller McCormick who always entered her Rolls-Royce to go to the Fortnightly, just across Bellevue Place from her palace.

In the above photograph of a gathering at The Cliff Dwellers in January 1913 are left to right, "A Line o' Type or Two" columnist Bert Leston Taylor, poet Edwin Markham, novelist Theodore Dreiser, and Hamlin Garland.

Chicago has had clubs whose members were far richer and more powerful than The Cliff Dwellers, but none has had members that were more truly distinguished. The primary force behind the club's founding was Hamlin Garland, the author of, among other works, the Midwestern masterpiece *A Son of the Middle Border.* In 1907 Garland approached his brother-in-law, the sculptor Lorado Taft, and others to form a club which would be, in Garland's words, "a home for all workers in the fine arts." The models were the Players and the National Arts clubs in New York. In 1909 the club took the name Cliff Dwellers from the title of Chicago novelist Henry B. Fuller's precedent-shattering study of urban life.

Perched atop Orchestra Hall at 220 South Michigan Avenue, the club's so-called "Kiva" is a restrained arts and crafts penthouse designed by member Howard Van Doren Shaw. A roll call of the members who have gathered there since its completion in 1909 would include names that have a lasting place in American cultural history. Among them are Carl Sandburg; George Ade; James Witcomb Riley; the illustrator, John T. McCutcheon; the children's poet, Eugene Field; the pioneering modern landscape architect, Jens Jenson; the composer, Leo Sowerby; and the "father" of Aspen, Colorado, Walter Paepcke.

Those who care for architecture are forever in The Cliff Dwellers' debt, for in Louis Sullivan's later years, when he was poor and almost forgotten, this founding member found a welcome in these rooms. "But he was at least safe in an armchair by a fireside. He was made a life member of The Cliff Dwellers. . . . It is one of the great virtues of that organization that it did this for him," wrote Frank Lloyd Wright, himself a member, in *Genius and Mobocracy.* To this day, the club preserves the desk where Sullivan wrote his *Kindergarten Chats.*

An historic moment at The Cliff Dwellers on March 11, 1915 (top) with Louis Sullivan, second from left, and on the far right Irving K. Pond, the architect who designed much of Hull House for Jane Addams.

The main lounge of The Cliff Dwellers about 1915 (above) with the architect of the club, Howard Van Doren Shaw, third from left, and the sculptor Lorado Taft seated in the chair to the right of the fireplace.

"Carroll Dowson had just joined South Shore Country Club . . . and was getting up in the world." Studs Lonigan's envy of Dowson's ability to "climb the social ladder," as expressed in James T. Farrell's *Judgement Day,* is accurate in its depiction of the status of the South Shore Country Club. The magnificent course on Lake Michigan at 7059 South Shore Drive drew its membership from the opulent residential thoroughfares of the South Side such as Grand and Drexel boulevards which were lined with the mansions of families like the Edward Morrises—he was the son of Nelson Morris, she was the daughter of Gustavus Swift.

The South Shore's first clubhouse, seen below in 1908, was superseded in 1916 by a luxurious four-story, Mediterranean-inspired structure designed by Marshall and Fox which was closely related in style to the firm's Edgewater Beach Hotel, completed the same year. When it opened, *The Upholsterer* magazine proclaimed it the most beautiful country club in the world.

At left is the South Shore's solarium with Adam-type decorations by Hasselgren Studios. Below is the airy classical grand ballroom, a majestic space created by Benjamin Marshall with details executed by W. P. Nelson and Company. The photograph of a luncheon overlooking the fairway at the South Shore in the 1920s (above) was taken about the time Carroll Dowson joined. The club closed at the beginning of the 1970s.

In the 1920s, just north of the Tribune Tower on Michigan Avenue, Chicago's Shriners commissioned some of the city's most exotic interiors to house their Medinah Club. Completed in 1929 and designed by Walter W. Alschlager, it was unadulterated Hollywood Spanish. The sense of a movie set is evident in the Medinah's Spanish Tea Court (left) in the ballroom (above) and in the swimming pool (below) beneath its handsome wood-beamed ceiling. The club fell on hard times during the Depression and the forty-five-story Medinah Club building became the Chicago Towers; it is now a hotel.

"The distinctive new rooms of the Tavern Club of Chicago show how . . . adaptable to club interiors is the modern art style of decoration," reported *Good Furniture* magazine in March 1929. Indeed, in the 333 North Michigan Avenue skyscraper home for a club which prided itself on the membership of architects such as John Holabird, John Wellborn Root, Jr., Philip Maher, and Noel Flint, the designers made a dramatic break with men's town clubs noted mainly for leather and dark wood paneling. The meticulous attention to detail by the decorators, Johns Hopkins of Holabird and Root, the club's architects, and Winold Reiss of New York, is evident in the gray fabric-covered walls of the foyer (above) striated with geometric patterns, which recall the designs of the Viennese Joseph Hoffmann, and in the copper Art Deco grill (left).

The delightful card room (left) was enlivened by vivid red, purple, and green murals by the Chicago artist and club member, William Welch. An intimate dining nook (above) was set off with a silver-tasseled, blue valance and draperies, while its gray banquettes had matching blue cushions.

The Tavern Club's striking modern solarium overlooking Michigan Avenue (below) provides an interesting contrast to that of the South Shore Country Club. It had natural stone walls and willow green reed furniture upholstered in bright blue. Only plants separated the solarium from the Palm Room. One of the Palm Room's tropical murals painted by club member John Norton may be seen on the right.

The Tavern Club was redecorated in its original spirit in 1937-38 by member Samuel Marx, but recent work has destroyed its unique Art Deco ambiance.

VIII PUBLIC SPACES

A city to be great must have not just great buildings, but buildings that express at once, both by their exteriors and in their interiors, that they are the centers of great business. By great business is meant the supreme concerns of man: justice and government, learning and the arts, and faith. If the edifices constructed to honor these concerns are noble and beautiful, men have a chance, at least intermittently, to rise above the relentless pressures of their daily lives.

Where the People Rule

Chicago's most impressive example of a public structure was the Federal Building constructed between 1898 and 1905 to house the city's main post office, the United States courts, and various government bureaus. The Roman-inspired edifice was designed by Henry Ives Cobb. The choice of Cobb was significant, as the leading French architectural journal, *La Construction Moderne,* noted in its issue of May 29, 1897: "When it was decided to erect a new post office in Chicago . . . its citizens had enough influence upon the Federal Government to induce Congress to commission a man of known reputation to design what would be a monumental structure and one that would be in keeping with the growth and prominence that city had attained." Cobb was, in fact, the first non-government architect since 1853 to design a United States post office.

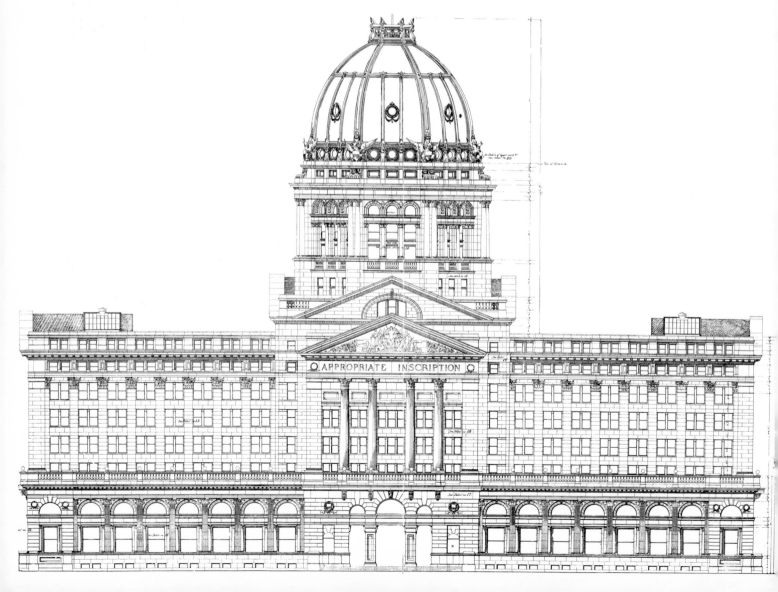

The massive classical Federal Building, a drawing of which is shown opposite, filled the block bounded by Adams, Jackson, Dearborn, and Clark streets and was crowned by a dome which soared sixteen stories above the pavement. The imperial panoply of the structure was considered fitting for a city whose self-confidence was caught perfectly by Henry B. Fuller in *The Cliff-Dwellers:* " . . . and we expect to be the financial center, and presently the political center, too—Chicago, plus New York and Washington."

The courtroom (below), like so

much else in the Federal Building, expressed the ideals of the Beaux-Arts architects who had triumphed at the Columbian Exposition held in Chicago in 1893, where, curiously, Cobb's Fisheries Building was one of the rare non-classical pavilions. Here Cobb has employed engaged Corinthian columns as well as murals and eagles to symbolize the grandeur of American law.

No cost was spared on the building's interior decoration and the bill came to more than $2,000,000. The rotunda (left) was of white and reddish-brown marble set off by gilded bronze.

The rotunda's floor was of brightly colored marble mosaic.

The edifice was filled with symbols of the patriotism which pervaded America at the turn-of-the-century. A doorknob (left) boldly bore a U. S.—or dollar sign—while the eagle in the decorative bronze grill of a doorway (right) seemed to proclaim America the heir of ancient Rome. This building, which gave a much needed sense of civic dignity to the Loop, was pulled down in 1965.

113

Fourteen years after the Great Fire of 1871, Chicago, after many delays and mounting costs which eventually totaled $5,000,000, inaugurated its grandiose new city hall. James J. Egan was chief architect. The City Council chamber, shown below during the 1907 swearing in of Mayor Fred A. Busse, was an ornate, highly theatrical Gilded Age interior planned by L. D. Cleveland, superintendent of buildings. It was in this chamber that the notorious "Gray Wolves" among the aldermen voted, for a price, the franchises that gave the ex-convict from Philadelphia, Charles T. Yerkes, control of Chicago's traction companies. The events were to be the basis of Theodore Dreiser's novel, *The Titan*.

Between 1908 and 1911 Egan's edifice was replaced by a block square classical building by Holabird and Roche. Its restrained wood-paneled City Council chamber is seen at right as it appeared in 1930. A series of ten murals by Frederic C. Bartlett, depicting events such as the Great Fire, filled the chamber with color. This room was ruined by a blaze in 1957 and what reemerged, under the guidance of city architect Paul Gerhardt, was an aggressively bland, pseudo-"modern" space that looked more like a broadcasting studio than the deliberative chamber of a free people. At right below, in this 1958 view of its dedication, former governor Adlai Stevenson is at far left on the podium and Mayor Richard J. Daley is fourth from left behind the microphones.

114

Vaults of Civilization

No Chicago interior more effectively dramatizes the importance of high civilization than the grand staircase of the Roman-style public library which opened in 1897 on Michigan Avenue at Washington Street. Designed by Charles A. Coolidge of the Boston firm of Shepley, Rutan, and Coolidge, it is a sumptuous late Victorian polychromed space of white Carrara marble set with rare green Connemara marble, mother-of-pearl, and semi-precious stones. The dazzling mosaics of glass, supplied by Louis Tiffany and finished in 1898, are the work of J. A. Holzer, an American pioneer in the form, who was associated with Tiffany and who is also responsible for the mosaics in the Marquette Building. They are in the Byzantine revival style popularized in the 1880s by Victoriem Sardou's highly-successful play *Theodora* which starred Sarah Bernhardt.

116

The library's furnishings—the specially designed pieces were supplied by the A. H. Andrews Company—were in the curving rococo style favored in the 1890s. Typical of them is the lion-footed bench at right. The decorative theme of many of the pieces was patriotic, as with the fierce eagle finial of the bench seen opposite below. The reason for this was not only because of contemporary patriotic fervor, but also because it was mandated by the fact that one of the purposes of the library was to provide a meeting place for the members of the Grand Army of the Republic. At right below is a trophy-crowned doorway in the second-floor lobby of the G.A.R.'s rooms, and below is one of the society's treasures, Pauline Dohn's copy of George P. A. Healy's portrait of Illinois' greatest son, Abraham Lincoln.

After a careful restoration by Holabird and Root, the building reopened in 1977 as the Chicago Public Library Cultural Center. Unfortunately, in the process of restoring the library, much of its wonderful old furniture disappeared.

"It was with a lightening of the heart, a feeling of throwing off the old miseries and old sorrows of the world, that she ran up the wide staircase to the pictures." Willa Cather's description in *The Song of the Lark* of what her heroine Thea Kronborg felt for the Art Institute is a tribute to its architecture as well as to its collections. Shepley, Rutan, and Coolidge planned a monumental staircase under a dome for their Beaux-Arts palace which opened for the 1893 Columbian Exposition, but financial problems intervened. Construction on the stairway (above) did not begin until 1910 and though it continued until 1913, the marble balustrades and the dome were never completed. The result is an unexpectedly modern-looking and undeniably powerful stairway that does indeed draw visitors up to the galleries above.

At left is the entrance hall of the Art Institute as it appeared when completed in 1894. (The light well has been covered.) From its incorporation in 1879 as the

Chicago Academy of Fine Arts—it received its present name in 1882—its supporters have never doubted the importance of art as a civilizing influence. Their hopes were expressed by Edgar Lee Masters in "Chicago":

But over the switch yard stands
    the Institute
Guarded by lions on the avenue,
Colossal lions standing for attack;
Between whose feet luminous
    and resolute
Children of the city passing
    through
To palettes, compasses, the
    demoniac
Spirit of the city shall subdue.

The Civic Opera House, part of a forty-five-story skyscraper on Wacker Drive, opened in the winter of 1929-30. It was designed by Graham, Anderson, Probst, and White and was the inspiration of utilities magnate Samuel Insull. Its auditorium (above), seating nearly 3,500 people, was the work of the designer Alfred Shaw. The original color scheme, with coral velvet hangings, coral mohair for the orchestra seats, and gold chairs with red and gold Italian damask in the boxes, as well as the decorative groups of gilded trumpets, was suggested by the painter Jules Guérin. This photograph, taken on

December 27, 1933, shows the house's thirty-one boxes that curved so slightly inward that they were said to have replaced the Diamond Horseshoe with the Golden Crescent.

The decor of the Civic Opera House was categorized by *Good Furniture* magazine in its March 1930 issue as "a modern adaptation of French Renaissance style." Whatever that might mean, the opera house certainly owed a debt to the chic French liners which then plied the Atlantic.

119

Where the People Worship

In *The Gothic Quest* of 1907, Ralph Adams Cram, the dean of American church architects, proclaimed that Gothic was the only style appropriate for a Christian church and described it as "less a method of construction than it is a mental attitude, the visualizing of a spiritual impulse." Certainly the style was not unknown to Chicagoans. The city's first brick church, St. James Protestant Episcopal, finished in 1837, had vague Gothic yearnings and these yearnings became more identifiable in that pre-fire survivor, the Congregational Church on Union Park. But these were only precursors and Chicago, heeding the call of Cram and the other architects who demanded historically accurate Gothic churches, was to construct a number of impressive monuments of that style, monuments that were, to quote Cram, "all glorious within."

A small gem of the Gothic revival was the Hibbard Memorial Chapel of old Grace Protestant Episcopal Church at 1439 South Wabash Avenue (right). Dedicated in 1906, the English perpendicular Gothic chapel was designed by Bertram Goodhue, an associate of Cram in the New York and Boston based firm of Cram, Goodhue, and Ferguson. The limestone and brick structure had a fine chestnut reredos. Grace Church, a favorite of Prairie Avenue society, and its Hibbard Chapel burned in 1915.

Among Chicago's most venerable examples of the Gothic revival is Holy Name Cathedral on North State Parkway, the seat of the Roman Catholic archdiocese of Chicago. Built to replace a cathedral destroyed in the Great Fire, Holy Name was dedicated in 1875 and was the work of the New York architect Patrick Charles Keely who designed hundreds of Roman Catholic churches. Keely's original interior, seen at left looking from the altar in this rare gravure, was in a form much favored by him: a preaching church, broad for its length, with a large unobstructed nave. Its details are reminiscent of the pointed Gothic of English cathedrals such as Salisbury. In a renovation completed in 1893 by Willett and Pashley, the church's original wooden piers were replaced by clustered ones of colored marble. The cathedral was extensively renovated in 1914 and again between 1968 and 1969 when much of its nineteenth-century decoration, which gave it both a sense of history and a certain charm, was destroyed.

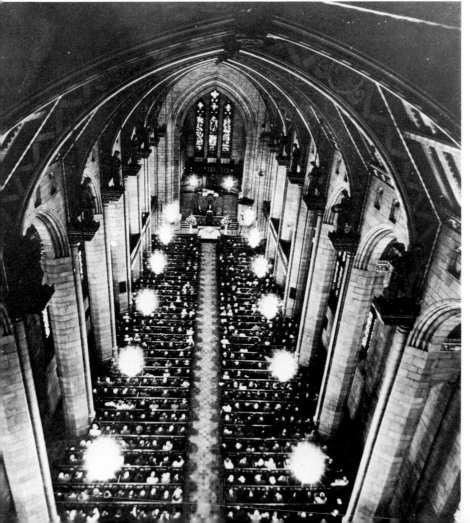

The city's most awesome Gothic interior is the vast Rockefeller Memorial Chapel at the University of Chicago (above). Although designed by Bertram Goodhue in 1918, it was not completed until 1928 after his death. The quality of the detail in Rockefeller Chapel is evident in the oak organ screen carved by Alois Lang of Oberammergau, Germany. Its central figure is Jubal whom Genesis calls "the father of all such as handle the harp and organ."

In the Fourth Presbyterian Church of 1912 on North Michigan Avenue (left) Chicago possesses an outstanding example of the work of Ralph Adams Cram himself, the architect of such Gothic tours de force as the nave of the Cathedral of St. John the Divine in New York, and the chapel at Princeton University. The church is in a freely adapted English Gothic style with a rich, polychromed ceiling decorated by Frederic C. Bartlett and stained glass windows by the renowned Charles Connick in handsome green and grisaille patterns. This photograph looking down the nave was taken in 1965 during the funeral of Marshall Field IV.

121

Gothic was by no means the only mode embraced by Chicago's houses of worship. The Roman Catholic Church always had a fondness for the classical, and in 1916 on the far North Side at the corner of Lunt Avenue and Paulina Street it dedicated St. Jerome's (above), one of the city's truly superb sanctuaries in that style. The architect responsible for the rich Italian Renaissance design was Charles H. Prindiville. Between 1931 and 1943 St. Jerome's was greatly enlarged and redecorated in a manner faithful to its original conception by John A. Mallin. With its dazzling display of marbles, its walls of gold mosaic, its heroic paintings, and its carved gold leaf ceiling, St. Jerome's would not be out of place in Rome.

For the Temple Isaiah on Hyde Park Boulevard (left) Alfred S. Alschuler, who had worked with Dankmar Adler, turned to Byzantine forms for inspiration. He was influenced in his choice by photographs of an ancient synagogue which had been excavated in Tiberias, Palestine, while he was designing the temple in 1923.

When photographs of Frank Lloyd Wright's Unitarian

Universalist Church of 1906 in Oak Park (above) were published in Europe they created a sensation. The reinforced concrete exterior was startling enough, but the cream-colored interior with green trim and natural oak molding spoke an entirely new architectural language. Though the basic form here is a Greek cross inscribed in a square, the architect dramatically broke with the past in this flat-roofed, cubist interior. For this liberal Unitarian congregation Wright created a sanctuary where space is all, where walls disappear, and where the outside is welcomed into the interior.

The temple that Wright's mentors, Sullivan and Adler, built at 3301 South Indiana Avenue for Kehilath Anshe Ma'ariv was revolutionary in its own way, for its barrel-vaulted hall (right) was ornamented with Sullivan's extraordinary designs. Adler's father, Rabbi Liebman Adler, was present when the temple was dedicated in 1891. It is now a church and the historic Jewish body—its name means Congregation of the Men of the West—is housed in Temple Isaiah (opposite).

The marble bar (above) with its gentlemen's cafe in the rear was one of the leading attractions of the post-fire Palmer House, designed by Charles Maldon Palmer. Potter Palmer, who was not, interestingly enough, related to the architect, was obsessed with the idea of proper lighting for his hotel. When it opened in 1873 almost every fixture was a special design by H. M. Wilmarth and Brother of Chicago, fabricated by Mitchell, Vance, and Company of New York. In the spring of 1882, Palmer began to have electric lights installed in his public rooms, making his hotel one of the nation's first to be so illuminated.

IX ROOMS TO REMEMBER

The pages of Chicago novels and the memoirs of Chicago writers are filled with the names of fondly remembered rooms. Willa Cather delighted in nourishing her heroines in the main dining room of the Auditorium Hotel, while Frank Norris usually managed to provide his characters with at least one repast at Kinsley's or the Grand Pacific. In 1963 in *Gaily, Gaily,* his recollections of the Chicago he had known as a tyro reporter a half century earlier, Ben Hecht wrote: "I sat in Henrici's restaurant with my dream of fair women . . . " On that particular occasion, alas, Hecht found the reality less alluring than the dream. It is to be hoped that he smothered his sorrow with a portion of Henrici's fine finnan haddie followed by a mouth-watering linzer tart. Henrici's was a room to remember.

This 1890s photograph shows that Potter Palmer wished to make sure that his patrons were never left in the dark, for his bar has gas and electric fixtures, as well as candles.

At right is a menu from the legendary time when a dollar was worth a dollar and a dinner cost a good deal less.

PALMER HOUSE GENTLEMEN'S CAFE
·DINNER·
Saturday, June 5, 1909
THE PALMER HOUSE, CHICAGO
From 12 M. to 3 P. M. and 5:30 P. M. to 7:30 P. M.

Blue Points............. 20   Little Neck Clams... 20

SOUP
Cream of Asparagus......... 15   Italian Paste...... 15

FISH
Baked Red Snapper, Wine Sauce............... 25
Parisian Potatoes

BOILED
Brisket of Beef, Horseradish Sauce............ 25

ROAST
Beef 30   Turkey, Cranberry Sauce.. 40
Loin of Pork, Apple Sauce...... 25

Broiled Quail on Toast 40   Broiled Plover on Toast.... 30

ENTREES
Breast of Lamb Breaded, with Peas 30
Fried Frog Legs, Tomato Sauce.. 30
Rice Fritters, Vanilla Flavor.. 15
Baked Pork and Beans................. 20

COLD
Lobster Salad.................... 30   Sliced Cucumbers............ 15
Salmon Mayonnaise........... 25   Celery 10
Spiced Oysters.................. 25   Dill Pickles.................... 5
Roast Beef... 30; with Potato Salad 40   Pickled Beets...... 5
Roast Chicken or Lamb with Lettuce or Potato Salad........ 40
Lettuce or Chicory Salad... 20   Melon Mangoes 10
Boiled Lobster, with Chow-chow or Chili Sauce...... 40

DESSERT
English Plum Pudding, Hard and Brandy Sauce..... 10
Apple Pie......................... 10   Mince Pie......................... 10
Cherry Pie 10   Lemon Custard Pie............ 10
Pies with Ice Cream......... 15   Peach Pie......................... 10
Benedictine Punch........... 10   Palmer House Ice Cream.... 10
Assorted Cakes................. 10

125

The ladies entrance on Monroe Street of the Palmer House of 1873 (above) was typical of those in fashionable hotels after the Civil War when women didn't use the main entrances. They also didn't sign the guest registers, which often included strong words beside the signatures.

At right is a never-before-reproduced stereopticon view of the post-fire Palmer House Restaurant. Potter Palmer personally supervised the decoration of this lavish circular room, which was surrounded by immense mirrors and illuminated from above through a glass dome held up by varicolored Ionic and Corinthian marble columns. The room's frescoes and its much-commented-upon tessellated floor were created by Italian workmen brought to Chicago for the project. The restaurant served hotel guests on the European plan, as well as patrons not staying at the Palmer House. There was a special Grand Dining Room for guests on the American plan.

The passing in 1962 of Henrici's at 71 West Randolph Street (right) was mourned by thousands. Though it seated 500 diners, architect and decorator August Fiedler achieved a sense of intimacy with the use of dark wood paneling and a richly carved cornice. When the room opened in 1894 frescoes filled the lighted circles of the ceiling. Because of its famed bakery which featured temptations such as German almond cake and chocolate eclairs, Henrici's was Diamond Jim Brady's favorite Chicago eatery.

This 1890s view (below) of the Hannah and Hogg bar in the Fisher Building at 343 South Dearborn Street illustrates what George Ade in *The Old-Time Saloon* called "the cathedral architecture" of some Windy City watering holes. Hannah and Hogg, a distilling and bottling company, owned a number of Chicago's most richly appointed saloons. The finest were adorned with bars of highly polished marble or onyx and had floors with mosaic sporting scenes. Like most, this one vanished in the 1920s during the drought brought on by Prohibition.

Chicago's German restaurants, past and present, are legion: Schlogl's, Vogelsang's, the dining room of the Kaiserhof Hotel, the Germania, and the Berghoff, to list some of the more famous. Few national groups have so packed their dining places with unabashed nostalgia for their homeland. The Old Heidelberg on West Randolph Street (above and center) grew out of a restaurant of the same name at the 1933 Century of Progress Exhibition. It was founded by Robert and Max Eitel of the family that owned the Bismarck Hotel. The picturesque setting, where one would not have been surprised to hear strains from *The Student Prince,* was by Graham, Anderson, Probst, and White. It has now fallen on less lyrical days. The playful facade has been desecrated and the restaurant houses a cafeteria and a fast food outlet.

No Chicago German restaurant was more famous than The Red Star Inn which opened in 1899 at North Clark Street and Germania Place. The Red Star featured a replica of a Bavarian chalet (far right above) complete with leaded bottle-glass windows and bierstube tables, which was used for private parties by notables such as Jules Rosenwald of Sears and Florenz Ziegfeld of the Follies. The old inn and its little chalet gave way to a housing project in 1970.

Another version of romantic north European architecture was the Stockyards Inn in the midst of the now vanished Union Stockyards at 41st and Halsted streets. A delightful English Tudor structure, it had originally been built by R. S. Lindstrom in 1912 and was extensively reconstructed after a fire in 1934 by A. Epstein and Associates. Its great banquet hall, seen at right shortly before it closed in December 1976, was decorated with portraits of famous Chicago cattlemen. The Stockyards Inn, with its 200 guest rooms, which had housed notables such as Dwight Eisenhower, its fourteen dining rooms, and four bars, was demolished in 1977.

One of the most pleasant amenities made possible by the skyscraper is the dining room in the clouds. Among the earliest promoters of this concept were Burnham and Root who created the twenty-two-story Masonic Temple of 1892 at the northeast corner of State and Randolph streets. The remnants of its roof garden are shown at right as the building was being demolished in 1939. It featured a restaurant and theatre and was topped by a glass-enclosed observatory. The 1906 photograph (opposite above) looking south down State Street from the Chicago River captures the Masonic Temple in its original glory.

An idea of the appearance of the interior of the Masonic Temple's roof garden may be gained from the illustration opposite below by John T. McCutcheon for one of George Ade's *Chicago Stories* titled "In the Roof Garden." The setting is the top of the Masonic Temple and the characters are two very up-to-date men-about-town, Ollie and Fred.

Behind the Masonic Temple's iron and steel skeleton looms the baroque dome of 35 East Wacker Drive. Originally the Jewelers Building, its unusual form was said by a real estate brochure to typify the goldsmith's art. The plans for this 1927 skyscraper (above), for which Thielbar and Fugard were the supervising architects, called for a spectacular grill on the thirty-ninth floor.

Skyscrapers did indeed make it possible to dine in the clouds, but man still longed to fly above them. In the 1920s and '30s designers like Norman Bel Geddes became fascinated with airplanes, airships, and airports as symbols of the streamlined world they hoped to bring into being. The distinguished

architect, Fritz August Breuhaus de Groot, for instance, was most proud of having designed the smoking-room of the German airship "Hindenburg." On May 20, 1933 the La Salle Hotel introduced its new roof garden (left) and named it The Hangar. Appropriately, the chief decoration was a huge mural of a

dirigible and airplanes flying above the modernistic buildings of the just-opened Century of Progress Exposition.

Benjamin Marshall's yellow stucco Edgewater Beach Hotel attempted to show just how *au courant* it was by adding a "hydro aeroplane" dock (above left) in the

1920s. Above is the Edgewater Beach's trellis-patterned Marine Dining Room, which, until the advent of Lake Shore Drive, overlooked the hotel's 1,000 feet of Lake Michigan beach front. Sadly, Chicago has lost both the Edgewater Beach and the La Salle hotels.

In the days when everyone traveled across the country by train, Chicago was where they changed from the Twentieth Century to the Super Chief. If the travelers happened to be cafe society or show business types looking for publicity, they most likely found time to drop in at the Pump Room of the Ambassador East Hotel. If they were celebrities of the ilk of the Duke and Duchess of Windsor or Bogart and Bacall or Judy Garland and Lassie they would be quickly ensconced in coveted booth one.

In the 1930s what became the Pump Room (left) was simply the dining room of the Ambassador East. The work of the Chicago designer and architect Samuel A. Marx, who was also responsible for much of the decoration of New York's Hotel Pierre, it was a fine Georgian period room in yellow, white, and green, lighted by Waterford crystal chandeliers and wall sconces.

In 1944, in order to attract more business and provide a dramatic stage set for restaurateur Ernie Byfield, the space (below) was transformed. It was named the Pump Room after a famed eighteenth-century gathering place

in the English spa of Bath. Marx, along with Noel Flint and C.W. Schonne, blocked the windows, covered the balustrades with tufted leather, and added booths and a bar. At right Pump Room employees, led by a young man in a feathered turban, parade with yuletide treats during the 1974 Christmas season. At right below a waiter in knee breeches—like the turban part of the room's decor—holds aloft skewers of flaming shish kebab. In 1976 the Pump Room, which was Chicago's El Morocco and Stork Club, became another room to remember.

SOURCES AND NOTES FOR ILLUSTRATIONS

Room, and the corridor known as Peacock Alley. *From:* The Inland Architect and News Record, *Vol. XL, No. 6*

8   The restaurant of the Blackstone Hotel. The hotel's original address was South Michigan Avenue and East Seventh Street. The restaurant overlooked Michigan Avenue, measured forty-eight by seventy-six feet and had a twenty-six-foot-high ceiling. The Blackstone's plan was considered a revolutionary advance in hotel planning and won a gold medal from the Illinois Chapter of the AIA in 1909. The restaurant at present retains little of its past grandeur. *From:* The American Architect, *June 29, 1910*

9   Lobby of the Stevens Hotel, now the Conrad Hilton, 720 South Michigan Avenue. The furniture in the Stevens, all American-made, was supplied by Marshall Field and Company and the carpets came from Carson, Pirie, Scott, and Company. On November 1, 1943, after serving for a year as an Air Force Technical Training School, the Stevens was returned to civilian use. The designer in charge of the hotel's refurbishing was Raymond Anthony Court, who had decorated the restaurants in New York's Rockefeller Center. This photograph, taken on July 2, 1959, shows the lobby prepared for the visit of Queen Elizabeth II of Britain four days later. *Private Collection*

Magnificence in the Loop

10   Palmer House hotel advertisement, 1877. The advertisement reflects the business community's concern for the growing power of the Greenback Party, which called for the free coinage of silver on a parity with gold and the suppression of national bank notes. *Private Collection*

10   Check-in lobby of the Palmer House hotel, State and Monroe streets. Some have attributed this edifice to John Van Osdel. Van Osdel was the architect of the Palmer House hotel that opened a few months before the Great Chicago Fire of 1871 and was consumed in that holocaust. Photograph by Kaufmann and Fabry, 1880s. *Courtesy of the Palmer House*

11   View of hallway in Palmer House, with entrance to the Grand Parlor on the right and doorway to bridal chamber at the far end. Stereopticon, 1880s. *Courtesy of the Rogers Collection, New York Historical Society*

11   Kitchen, Palmer House hotel. Engraving, 1883. *Private Collection*

12   Main lobby, Palmer House hotel. Photograph by Hedrich-Blessing, 1920s. *Courtesy of Hedrich-Blessing*

12-13   Detail of main lobby ceiling, painted in Italian Renaissance style. *From:* The Architect, *July 1926*

12-13   View of the Empire Room, 1950s. The room opened as a supper club on May 1, 1933 with the ballroom dance team of Veloz and Yolanda. On its last night, January 19, 1976, the entertainment was provided by Phyllis Diller. *Courtesy of the Palmer House*

13   Lobby of the ballroom, Palmer House hotel. Photograph by Hedrich-Blessing, 1926. *Courtesy of Hedrich-Blessing*

14   Souvenir program of Chicago Yale Association dinner held at the Grand Pacific Hotel, December 27, 1889. The menu, in addition to blue point oysters and sirloin of beef, featured something called "Siberian Punch." *Courtesy of Lila Hotz Tyng*

14   Lobby of the Grand Pacific Hotel. Engraving, 1877. *Courtesy of the New York Public Library*

14   Cross section of the Grand Pacific Hotel. *From:* The Land Owner, *March 1871, courtesy of the Newberry Library*

14   Ground floor plan of the Grand Pacific Hotel. *From:* The Land Owner, *March 1871, courtesy of the Newberry Library*

15   Bar of the Grand Pacific Hotel. Photograph taken in the 1890s. *Private Collection*

15   Exterior view of the Grand Pacific Hotel, corner of Clark Street and Jackson Boulevard, 1880s. *Courtesy of the Chicago Historical Society*

16   Lobby, La Salle Hotel. All of the hotel's furnishings were supplied by the Pooley Furniture Company whose Chicago studios were located in the Fine Arts Building. Photograph, 1909. *Private Collection*

16   View looking north on La Salle Street with the La Salle Hotel at Madison Street, on the left. The temporary plaster arch was erected to honor the Grand Encampment of the Knights Templar. Photograph, August 1910. *Courtesy of the Chicago Historical Society*

17   Details of side elevation, Grand Ballroom or Banquet Hall, La Salle Hotel. Drawing, 1908. *Private Collection*

17   Ballroom or Banquet Hall, La Salle Hotel. The tunnel-shaped ballroom was very popular at the beginning of the twentieth century. New York's Astor Hotel of 1904, by Clinton and Russell, had a similar ballroom. Photograph, 1909. *Private Collection*

Northern Lights

18   Lobby of the Edgewater Beach Hotel, Sheridan Road at Berwyn Avenue. A high-rise apartment building now occupies the site of the once-fashionable hotel. Photograph, 1920s. *Private Collection*

19   Dining room of the Pearson Hotel, 190 East Pearson Street. Photograph by Hedrich-Blessing, 1920s. *Courtesy of Hedrich-Blessing*

19   Exterior of the Edgewater Beach Hotel showing entrance and motor bus. Postcard, 1921. *Courtesy of the Chicago Historical Society*

20   Queen Marie of Roumania's reception room, the Lake Shore Drive Hotel, 181 East Lake Shore Drive. The architects of the hotel were Fugard and Knapp. International Newsreel Photograph, November, 1926. *Private Collection*

20   Queen Marie of Roumania's bedroom, Lake Shore Drive Hotel. Photograph, November 1926. *Private Collection*

20   Eleanor Medill Patterson, granddaughter of Joseph Medill Patterson, founder of the *Chicago Tribune*, at the Lake Shore Drive Hotel. Eleanor "Cissy" Patterson was to make a reputation for herself in the world of journalism as editor-in-chief of the *Washington Herald*. Photograph, 1924. *Private Collection*

21   Exterior of the Plaza Hotel, northeast corner of Clark Street and North Avenue. Photograph, turn-of-the-century. *Courtesy of The Art Institute of Chicago*

21   Lobby ceiling of the Plaza Hotel. Photograph by Harold Allen, June 5, 1964. *Courtesy of Harold Allen*

53 View of bay in drawing room of the Edith Rockefeller-McCormick mansion. On the desk in the center of the photograph is one of Mrs. McCormick's most highly prized Oriental artworks, an important Chinese figure of the T'ang period. Photograph, December 1933. *Private Collection*

54 The fabled Empire Room in the McCormick mansion, which was filled with furniture and objects that had belonged to Napoleon I. The contents of the house were auctioned off in December 1933 to help pay Mrs. McCormick's debts. Photograph, 1920s. *Private Collection*

54 Portrait of Franklin MacVeagh. MacVeagh, who was born in 1837 in Pennsylvania, graduated from Columbia Law School and practiced law for a time. He moved to Chicago for his health, unlikely as that might seem, and went into the wholesale grocery business. He was active in feeding people after the fire of 1871. In time, Franklin MacVeagh and Company became one of the largest wholesale grocery firms in the United States. Photograph, 1909. *Private Collection*

54 Portrait of Emily Eames MacVeagh. Emily MacVeagh was a niece of the wife of the distinguished Chicago jurist, John Dean Caton. Photograph, 1909. *Private Collection*

54 Interior view in the MacVeagh house looking into the conservatory from the dining room. Conservatories, made possible by the easy availability of iron and glass, were a rage among the Victorian upper middle and upper classes. In a city like Chicago with its hard winters they provided a delightful bit of greenery during the gray months which stretch from November to April. Photograph, 1890s. *Courtesy of The Art Institute of Chicago*

54 Exterior of the Franklin MacVeagh house, 103 Lake Shore Drive. The address gives no clear idea of the location of the house, since Lake Shore Drive has since been renumbered. The house, in fact, stood just north of the Potter Palmer castle at Lake Shore Drive and Schiller Street. Photograph, 1890s. *Courtesy of The Art Institute of Chicago*

55 First floor plan of Franklin MacVeagh house. Drawing, about 1883. *Private Collection*

55 Main doorway of the MacVeagh house, Schiller Street. Photograph, 1890s. *Private Collection*

56 Interior of the ballroom or music room of the Franklin MacVeagh house. The MacVeagh's musical evenings were famous. It is not unlikely that this is one of the rooms where Isadora Duncan danced when she began performing in private houses in Chicago in the 1890s. Photograph, 1890s. *Courtesy of The Art Institute of Chicago*

57 View from main stairway towards second story landing and into the hall of Potter Palmer castle. Photograph, about 1890. *Courtesy of The Art Institute of Chicago*

58 Carriage at entrance to Potter Palmer castle, 1350 Lake Shore Drive. By the 1890s fashionable Chicagoans had replaced their Negro and Scandinavian servants with English ones. English coachmen and butlers, in particular, were sought with the same fervor that was expended on the search for Ming vases. Photograph, 1890s. *Private Collection*

58 Original ground floor plan of the Potter Palmer castle. *From:* Illinois Society of Architects Monthly Bulletin, *January-February, 1946*

58-59 Library of the Potter Palmer castle. The enormous gas chandeliers made it possible to read a book quite easily, something that was a rarity in most nineteenth-century libraries after dark. They were soon replaced by electric lamps scattered throughout the room. Photograph, about 1890. *Courtesy of The Art Institute of Chicago*

59 Portrait of Mrs. Potter Palmer by F. Holland Day. Platinum print, about 1890. *Courtesy of the Alfred Stieglitz Collection, the Metropolitan Museum of Art, New York*

60 Dining room of the Potter Palmer castle. The portrait on the far wall is of Mrs. Palmer. There was one of Mr. Palmer at the other end of the sideboard. Photograph, about 1890. *Courtesy of The Art Institute of Chicago*

60 Drawing room of the Potter Palmer castle. Photograph, about 1890. *Courtesy of The Art Institute of Chicago*

61 Picture gallery of Potter Palmer castle, looking into main gallery from the east gallery. The galleries went through a number of fairly complete redecorations. This shows them in their final state after Mrs. Palmer's death. Photograph taken after 1920. *Courtesy of The Art Institute of Chicago*

61 Drawing room of the Potter Palmer castle. View of room after it was redecorated for the Potter Palmer IIs by David Adler. Photograph taken after 1920. *Courtesy of the Chicago Historical Society*

Houses of Talent

62 Portrait of the second Mrs. Marshall Field. Though she had long been friendly with Field, the second Mrs. Field had to wait until her husband Arthur Caton died before she could marry him. Arthur Caton died in 1904. The marriage to Field was a short one; he died in 1906. *From:* Elite, *January 4, 1902*

62 View of hall, Marshall Field house, 1905 Prairie Avenue. *From:* Artistic Houses, *1883. Courtesy of The Art Institute of Chicago*

63 Portrait of Marshall Field. Photograph, 1890s. *Courtesy of Marshall Field and Company*

63 Library of Marshall Field house. *From:* Artistic Houses, *1883. Courtesy of The Art Institute of Chicago*

64 Library of the Edward E. Ayer house, 2 East Banks Street. The house contained some notable art glass, some of which can be seen in the window at left. The ceiling was originally elaborately stenciled. Photograph by Harold Allen, June 24, 1964. *Courtesy of Harold Allen*

64 Portrait of John Wellborn Root. Photograph, 1870s. *Private Collection*

65 Entrance hall with fireplace, Edward E. Ayer house. Photograph by Harold Allen, June 24, 1964. *Courtesy of Harold Allen*

66 Library of the Martin A. Ryerson house, 4851 Drexel Boulevard. Photograph taken after 1906. *Courtesy of The Art Institute of Chicago*

66 Exterior of Ryerson house. Photograph taken after 1906. *Courtesy of the Art Institute of Chicago*

67 Mrs. Ryerson's bedroom on the second floor showing a

Claude Monet "Water Lilies" next to fireplace. Photograph taken after 1906. *Courtesy of The Art Institute of Chicago*

67   Black and white reproduction of Claude Monet's "Water Lilies" of 1906. It is part of the Mr. and Mrs. Martin A. Ryerson Collection now in The Art Institute of Chicago. *Courtesy of The Art Institute of Chicago*

67   Mr. and Mrs. Martin A. Ryerson with Claude Monet at Giverny outside Paris where his famed "Water Lilies" series was painted. From a Ryerson family album now in the Ryerson Library of The Art Institute of Chicago. Photograph taken shortly before the outbreak of World War I. *Courtesy of The Art Institute of Chicago*

68   Exterior of William O. Goodman house, 5026 Greenwood Avenue, with William O. Goodman in a buggy in front of it. Photograph, 1890s. *Courtesy of Marjorie Goodman Graff*

68   Cover of one-act comedy, "The Hero of Santa Maria," written by Kenneth Sawyer Goodman and Ben Hecht. The play was first presented by the Washington Square Players at the Comedy Theatre, New York, on February 12, 1917. It was published by Frank Shay in New York in 1920. *Private Collection*

68   Entrance hall of the William O. Goodman house. This and the other photographs of the Goodman house on Greenwood Avenue are from a family album in the possession of Mrs. Robert D. Graff, who was Marjorie Goodman, granddaughter of William O. Goodman and daughter of Kenneth Sawyer Goodman. Photograph, 1890s. *Courtesy of Marjorie Goodman Graff*

68   Sofa in the William O. Goodman house. Photograph, 1890s. *Courtesy of Marjorie Goodman Graff*

69   Dining room in the William O. Goodman house, Greenwood Avenue. As central heating usurped the essential purpose of the fireplace it became an object to be beautified. This one, typically, is adorned with oriental porcelain and a pair of imported Italian bronze andirons. Photograph, 1890s. *Courtesy of Marjorie Goodman Graff*

69   Bedroom in the William O. Goodman house, Greenwood Avenue. Photograph, 1890s. *Courtesy of Marjorie Goodman Graff*

70   Drawing room of the William O. Goodman house, 1353 Astor Street. From a family album of the Goodman's Astor Street house. Photograph, about 1914. *Courtesy of Marjorie Goodman Graff*

70   Exterior of the Goodman Astor Street house. The house is now known as the Court of the Golden Hand. From a family album. Photograph, about 1914. *Courtesy of Marjorie Goodman Graff*

V PRAIRIE PAVILIONS AND CASTLES IN THE AIR

Villas

71   The first verse of William Asbury Keyon's poem makes it quite clear that he did not care for cities:
    Oh, some may chose the forest glade,
    And some may love the sea,
    Others may seek the city's din:
    But none of these for me.
He also obviously didn't have any great liking for woods or the ocean, which should have made him very happy in Illinois.

71   View of the front porch of the John Farson house, 217 Home Avenue, Oak Park. This was perhaps the most perfect of George W. Maher's houses. Its sense of carefully ordered substantiality made it a model for houses of the prosperous classes throughout the Midwest. Photograph, about 1900. *Courtesy of The Art Institute of Chicago*

72   Garden front of the Harold Fowler McCormick house, Villa Turicum, Lake Forest. The exact meaning of "Turicum" is obscure. One guess is that it refers to the Latin word for the scent of incense burning. Photograph, 1920s. *Private Collection*

72-73   Drawing room of the McCormick villa with the Pompeiian Room opening on the right. The marble throughout the house was the finest that could be obtained in Italy. When this photograph was taken the house was already a ruin and had a $160,000 tax lien on it. Photograph, 1947. *Private Collection*

73   First floor plan of the McCormick house. Art critic Royal Cortissoz said of the plan that it was "an Italian, but not in the smallest degree exotic, design." *From: Monograph of the Work of Charles A. Platt, by Royal Cortissoz, 1913*

73   Pompeiian Room of the McCormick house. The photograph was taken as the contents of the house were being auctioned off a year after Edith Rockefeller-McCormick's death. The woman in the picture is not a member of the family. Photograph, 1934. *Private Collection*

74   Main facade of Mrs. Morse C. Ely's house, Lake Forest. Photograph, 1923. *Courtesy of The Art Institute of Chicago*

75   Entrance hall of the Ely house. Photograph, 1923. *Courtesy of The Art Institute of Chicago*

74-75   First floor plan of the Albert D. Lasker house, Lake Forest. *From: David Adler by Richard Pratt, M. Evans and Company, New York, 1970*

74-75   Drawing room of the Albert D. Lasker house. Photograph by Hedrich-Blessing, 1930s. *Courtesy of Hedrich-Blessing*

75   Hall of Albert D. Lasker house. Photograph by Hedrich-Blessing, 1930s. *Courtesy of Hedrich-Blessing*

Apartments

76   Arthur Dana Wheeler in his apartment at the Mentone Apartments, Erie and Dearborn streets. Photograph, April 1891. *Courtesy of the Chicago Historical Society*

76   Exterior of the Mentone Apartments. Photograph, 1891. *Courtesy of the Chicago Historical Society*

77   Exterior of the Pullman Building, Michigan Avenue at Adams Street. Drawing, early 1880s. *Private Collection*

77   Interior of covered entrance court of the Pullman Building, 79 East Adams Street. Photograph by Harold Allen, June 1956. *Courtesy of Harold Allen*

78   Dining room of the George Woodruff apartment, 1500 Lake Shore Drive. The room was said to have the feeling of the fourteenth century. The walnut chairs were upholstered in brown leather. Photograph, 1930. Gift of D. C. Watson. *Courtesy of The Art Institute of Chicago*

VI TWO STREETS

State: Emporiums of Delight

La Salle: Halls of Commerce

VII CLUBLAND

Chicago Hotel complex. Photograph, 1920s. *Courtesy of the Library of Congress*

110   Foyer of the Tavern Club, 333 North Michigan Avenue. Photograph by Tebbs and Knell, 1929. *Private Collection*

110   Decorative copper grill in the Tavern Club. Photograph by Tebbs and Knell, 1929. *Private Collection*

110-111   Card room in the Tavern Club. The design of the chairs was appropriate to their use. Photograph by Henry Fuermann and Sons, 1929. *Private Collection*

111   Dining nook overlooking Michigan Avenue in the Tavern Club. Photograph by Tebbs and Knell, 1929. *Private Collection*

111   Solarium of the Tavern Club. Photograph by Henry Fuermann and Sons, 1929. *Private Collection*

VIII   PUBLIC SPACES
Where the People Rule

112   The Dearborn Street elevation of the United States Post Office and Court House, Dearborn, Adams, Jackson, and Clark streets. Note the "appropriate inscription" beneath the pediment. The Federal Building which replaced this structure is a distinguished skyscraper on the same site, but it is without any sense of civic dignity. Drawing, 1897. *Private Collection*

113   Detail of interior of rotunda in Federal Building. Photograph, early 1960s. *Private Collection*

113   Courtroom in Federal Building. This was the courtroom of Judge Julius Hoffman. Photograph, early 1960s. *Private Collection*

113   Doorknob in Federal Building. Photograph, early 1960s. *Private Collection*

113   Bronze grill of a doorway with an eagle in Federal Building. Photograph, early 1960s. *Private Collection*

114   City Council chamber in post-fire City and County Building, La Salle, Clark, Randolph, and Washington streets. The scene is the swearing in of Chicago Mayor Fred A. Busse. Busse, a Republican, was later accused of having stock in companies doing business with the city. Photograph by George D. Lawrence, 1907. *Courtesy of the Library of Congress*

114-115   City Council chamber in the Holabird and Roche designed City and County Building of 1908. The sombre grandeur of the room relates it to the paneled public rooms of the La Salle Hotel, completed by the firm the same year the City and County Building opened. Photograph, January 11, 1930. *Private Collection*

114-115   The same City Council chamber is here being rededicated after a fire. On the podium next to former Governor Stevenson is the late Paul Angle, director of the Chicago Historical Society. Photograph, March 4, 1958. *Private Collection*

Vaults of Civilization

116   View of grand staircase in the Chicago Public Library, Michigan Avenue and Washington Street. The dome above may be made of glass supplied by Louis Tiffany. It now covers what is known as "the civic reception center." The choice of mosaics rather than murals to decorate the library was a pragmatic one dictated by the fact that, with the Illinois Central tracks just across Michigan Avenue, the site of the library was a particularly dirty one. Mosaics can be washed. Stereopticon, 1899. *Courtesy of the Library of Congress*

116   Eagle head finial on a bench in the Chicago Public Library. Photograph, 1972. *Private Collection*

117   Bench in the Chicago Public Library. Not only did most of the library's splendid furniture vanish during the building's restoration, but so did most of its fine mosaic flooring, under a sea of carpeting. Photograph, 1972. *Private Collection*

117   View of one of the Grand Army of the Republic rooms in the Chicago Public Library. The rooms house an interesting collection of Civil War Relics. Photograph, 1972. *Private Collection*

117   A doorway in a Grand Army of the Republic room in the Chicago Public Library. Photograph, 1972. *Private Collection*

118   Main stairway, The Art Institute of Chicago, Michigan Avenue at Adams Street. One of the reasons for the stairway's curiously modern look is that the pedestals to carry clustered columns were put in place, but the columns themselves were never raised. The unadorned pedestals have an almost Art Deco appearance. Still on display at The Art Institute is Jules Breton's "The Song of the Lark" which meant so much to Thea Kronborg and gave Willa Cather the title of her novel. Photograph, 1920s. *Courtesy of The Art Institute of Chicago*

118   Main entrance hall, Art Institute of Chicago. Plaster casts of famous statues, as seen here in abundance, were a major item of display in American museums in the nineteenth century. They were considered educational, and, of course, they helped fill what were still comparatively empty galleries. Photograph, 1906. *Courtesy of The Art Institute of Chicago*

119   View of auditorium of the Civic Opera House. The construction of the Civic Opera House sounded the death knell of the Auditorium as a hall for grand opera. This was the opening night and, for gentlemen, white tie and tails were still considered the only appropriate dress. The opera given was "Tosca." Photograph, December 27, 1933. *Courtesy of the* Daily Times, *Field Enterprises*

Where the People Worship

120   View of Holy Name Roman Catholic Cathedral, North State Parkway, looking down the nave from the altar. The interior has been greatly changed from the way architect Patrick Charles Keely designed it. Keely, born in Ireland about 1820, also designed the Roman Catholic cathedrals in Boston, Massachusetts; Providence, Rhode Island; and Erie, Pennsylvania. He died in Brooklyn in 1896. Gravure, before 1890. *Courtesy of the Chicago Historical Society*

120   Interior, Hibbard Memorial Chapel, Grace Protestant Episcopal Church, 1439 South Wabash Avenue. The chapel was named for William G. Hibbard, a partner in the important hardware firm of Hibbard, Spencer, Bartlett, and Company. It was given by his wife, Lydia

IX   ROOMS TO REMEMBER

Maxfield Parrish's painting, based on the famed Mother Goose rhyme "Sing-a-Song-o'-Sixpence" which adorned the Sherman House hotel's Celtic Room, was one of Chicago's most delightful public murals. It had been commissioned in 1910 from the popular illustrator for the Holabird and Roche-designed hostelry at Clark and Randolph streets. This was the fourth Chicago hotel to bear the Sherman House name. The hotel closed in February 1973, and this photograph was taken on April 19, the first day of the auction in which its contents were dispersed. The charming painting brought $25,000. (Private Collection)